# SACRED SPACE

KERRIE ERWIN

# SACRED SPACE

## FINDING HARMONY WITH FENG SHUI

Love & Write book
Published by Love & Write Publishing
PO Box 252
Summer Hill NSW 2130
Australia

www.loveandwrite.com.au



A copy of this publication can be found in the National Library of Australia.

Edited by Sage Written Word
Cover Design by Farrah Careem
Typeset by Typeskill

Printed in Australia

ISBN 978-0-9923070-8-0

10 9 8 7 6 5 4 3

"The basic sources of happiness are a good heart, compassion and love. If we have these mental attitudes, even if we are surrounded by hostility, we feel little disturbance. On the other hand, if we lack compassion and our mental state is filled with anger or hatred, we will not have peace."

DALAI LAMA

# DEDICATION

This book is dedicated to everyone in the world who knows what they want, but is not sure how to get there. It's for everyone that would love to live their life to the fullest and create their own dreams.

Let me show you how to clear the blockages in your home and life to create balance and harmony.

With utmost blessings, love and respect to my beloved family, friends and all the people I have had the greatest pleasure of crossing paths with in the past, present and future.

With Heartfelt Gratitude,
Love and Blessings,

Kerrie Jean Erwin xxx

# CONTENTS

# INTRODUCTION

## *Manifest The Life You Desire*

Have you ever wondered why things never go right for you in your life? Why you are constantly lacking energy? Why you feel stuck and no matter what you do in life, you never seem to get ahead? Do you feel you attract bad luck?

If this is how you think and see yourself, it's time to make a change. Now is the time to take action and become the creator of the life you want.

By taking personal responsibility and clearing the negative energy in your home, you can change your life forever and bring more peace and fulfillment into your life. This process will not only make you happier, healthier and more prosperous than you could ever imagine, but the energy will also completely shift around you, bringing in more positive experiences.

Once you have done this, your life, without a doubt, will dramatically change in the most incredible ways imaginable, and you can sit back and watch as your hopes, wishes and dreams finally become a reality.

## LIKE ATTRACTS LIKE

The first step is *positive thinking*. The power of positive thinking is an incredible force. Your body, mind and emotions are made up of energy. The energy is designed to flow in and out, like your breath, but sometimes it can get stuck. Energy can have a positive or negative charge. The law of attraction is based on the concept that like attracts like, that positive energy attracts positive energy. If you can train your mind to think positive thoughts, you will attract more positive energy into your life.

Positive thinking takes practice. Start by observing your own self-talk, by looking in the mirror and being aware of what you think. If it's negative, replace it with something positive. As you go about your day be aware of your thoughts and attitudes. If you catch yourself thinking something negative, sweep it away and replace it with something positive. Positive thinking is not about ignoring the more challenging aspects of life, it's about approaching all situations in a positive and productive way.

> *"Whether you think you can, or you think you can't — you're right."*
>
> *Henry Ford*

Negative energies can also get stuck in your home. During my many years of experience as an energy worker, I have seen thousands of cases of people improving their life by using the ancient art of feng shui to get rid of unwanted spirits. By clearing stuck negative energy in the home, you can attract positive energy into your household, which in turn will impact every aspect of your life.

## LETTING GO

We live in a consumer-based society where we are encouraged to measure our wealth by what we possess. The items we accumulate are meant to enhance our quality of life, but when they are not used, and are piled and squashed into sections of our home and office, they create blocked energy and clutter. When something no longer has a place in your space, it needs to go. It's not a clever idea to stockpile large quantities of appliances and trivial entertainment items because those old unused items block new energy and opportunities from entering your life. Your home and office need to be clean and functional so you can work more effectively, think clearly and focus on what it is you are meant to do.

It's not only your home and office that needs to be cleared of things that no longer serve you. Worn-out friendships or relationships that no longer help you could be the thing holding you down. Once you take the time and effort to look at yourself and your surroundings in a loving and honest way, are able let go of negative thoughts and energy, bad habits or situations, and clutter around the home and office that no longer serves you, you will be able to move onto the next stage of your life.

Learning how to work with energy can bring more peace, harmony, and fulfillment into your life. The benefits of understanding how to harness positive energy are numerous.

* Finding that you love yourself, your family and your friends.

* Enjoying what you do.

* Nothing can stop you once you understand energy.

* Trusting your instincts.

* Not being afraid of change.

* Having the faith, hope and drive to give everything a go.

* Inspiring others to believe in themselves.

# CHAPTER 1

## *Clearing Your Space*

The practice of feng shui originated in China thousands of years ago, where it was used to identify and create places where communities would flourish. Feng shui means *wind-water* and it is used to ensure that people live in harmony with their surroundings. Feng shui is also referred to as the ancient art of *placement* because it focuses on orienting things like furniture, colours, and room locations to balance the *chi* (energy) in the home or office. There are many different methods and interpretations of feng shui, and as such, I believe you should trust your own instincts and use common sense when it comes to choosing the tips and tools that work for you.

What I have found is that by understanding and implementing the basic principles of feng shui, you can create real magic in your life. Feng shui is a starting point for change; it opens doorways to positive experiences by balancing the energy in the home and creating good fortune for its inhabitants.

Unnecessary clutter in your space will impede the flow of energy in your home causing blockages. A blockage of energy will slow *down* the natural chi energies in your space and the free flow of universal energy. This will have physical consequences like tiredness, a lack of awareness, discomfort, and the energy in the space will feel heavy and unpleasant to live in. The good thing is you don't have to move or spend too much money to make changes. Just like spring-cleaning, but on an energetic level, space clearing releases negative energy and encourages positive energy to enter your life.

The more time and energy you spend tuning your awareness into your space and home, the better you and your family will feel. You are not only creating peace and harmony, but inviting success into your world. As I always say, if your intention is to create a safe and nurturing haven in your home, then you are also creating a strong foundation in the world for you and your family. By opening up to your own intuitive feelings, you will know if something does not feel right in any area or space in your home. You will be able to change this with the fundamental principles used in feng shui.

My inner wisdom has taught me that you can live anywhere in the world and you don't have to be a millionaire to feel happy. Peace and love is free here on earth. If you have a lovely home, which is ordered and feels good without the unnecessary clutter which creates chaos, your life, in general, will usually go well. Whatever makes *you* feel good is always the best way to go. If you are having problems in your life, or would just like a change, begin by clearing your home, office or space. This, without doubt, will clear blockages, shape up your life, and certainly get you going. So why not take a leap of faith? Trust your inner knowing and make the changes today.

When I work in homes, shops or offices, the space I am working in will always talk to me and give me information of a psychic nature. When I tell people this they are generally not convinced, but once they see me work they are amazed. Every living thing on the planet is made up of energy. People who are sensitive and open to their feelings will know this as well. If we all learnt to open ourselves up to trust our own innate abilities, our intuitive feelings would improve and we would be able to work with our gifts more often.

Wherever people have been or lived, they will always leave a massive amount of good and bad energy, or vibes, which is easy to detect on a psychic level. For example, if people in a home have argued, or there has been violence, they will always leave behind some negative energy that will affect the new people that move in. Unfortunately, the bad energy will stay and the new owners will feel this and be undoubtedly affected on some level. How many times have you walked into a space or house and wished you could get out of there as fast as possible?

The solution, of course, is simple. Whenever this happens you don't have to leave or find another space, you just need to change the energy by burning or smoking out the room with some sage. This automatically dissipates, cleans, and clears the build-up of negative or bad energy. You can also use dried gum leaves, or even mix the two together by placing them in a metal or stone bowl and burning them, allowing the smoke to do its thing and cleanse the room. Later on, when the energy is clear and you have opened all of your windows to allow the smoke to go out, you may want to enhance your space with some relaxing aromatherapy oils like lavender, rose, or frankincense.

Once you have completed these simple tasks, your space will feel better as the energy in the room will be lighter. This brings in peace, harmony, and balance to your life, and from there, you can pick out certain *cures* for each section of your home to enhance the positive energy.

## CLEAR OUT THE CLUTTER

Clearing out the clutter sounds simple enough but it is actually hard to do. Do you feel stuck in your life? Do things seem to go wrong all the time for no apparent reason? Are you wanting to make changes in your life, but you have no idea how or where to start? The answer is simple. Start by clearing all the clutter from your home and life to make way for new energies to come in. This means letting go of old and worn-out contracts with people, and setting boundaries by clearing out your home.

Your home is your foundation in life. When it is in harmony it is a wonderful base to work from to make your dreams a reality. By doing this simple, easy, and life-changing exercise you can bring changes into your life for the better. I can't tell you how many shocked, bewildered, and puzzled faces I have seen over the years when I have told my clients that if they are serious about making real changes in their lives, then they have to get rid of the past and their collections of beloved things stashed in every nook and cranny of their home.

Take a deep breath, be brave and just let it all go. You will find as soon as you begin to do this, you will feel freer and lighter and empowered to make decisions about the new you in every aspect of your life. Clutter only creates blockages and stale, worn-out, negative energies in your home. By simply clearing your space you can actually change your life in a big way. I call it creating magic and alchemy in your home and life.

Begin by clearing out all of your clutter in your home or working space. This means everything, so consider starting with these items.

## OLD CLOTHES

All the clothes you have stuffed in your cupboards and drawers that you are never going wear again have got to go. Give away your unwanted things to a charity as there are many people out there who could certainly use them. Often, it is better to give away your clothes and accessories to strangers as I have found friends and loved ones do not appreciate them as much.

An example of this is when a really good friend of mine, Tula, made an important lifestyle change and decided she no longer wanted to go to nightclubs anymore. Over the years, her extremely late nights and dysfunctional friends had begun to cause her too many headaches and problems as they clashed with her new and exciting interest in yoga and nutrition. Her new interests made her feel a whole lot better and got rid of her depression. She knew she had to let this part of her life go, so she slowly and very painfully packed up dozens and dozens of bags of very expensive and fabulous clothes, shoes, and accessories.

Once she had done this, she rang up her sister-in-law and asked if her younger daughters wanted them. They, of course, could not believe their luck and were overjoyed. They jumped at the chance of picking up some amazing clothes and this made Tula feel good. A couple of weeks later, my good friend rang her sister-in-law again and could not believe her ears when the sister-in-law told her she had to throw everything in the bin as they smelt. Politely putting the phone down, Tula made a mental note of never giving anything to her jealous and cold hearted sister-in-law again.

## OLD FAVOURITES

Old and worn-out shoes, thongs, slippers, hats, odd socks, scarves, gloves, pyjamas and underwear, which may have been expensive or comfortable in their heyday, need to go if they are past their use-by date. It always amazes me how much stuff people store in their cupboards that never gets used.

## OLD MAKEUP

Sure, it might have looked good once, but do you really need to wear the eyeshadow that you wore years ago? Check out the use-by date as well because your well-loved products may be out of date. This can cause havoc with your skin or give you an eye infection. Mascaras should be replaced every three months and eye shadows, eye pencils, foundations, and lipsticks should be tossed after two years.

## OLD PAPERS

Get into your desk, cupboards, and drawers and start to go through all old papers. Throw out any papers that you no longer need. Also, throw out the newspapers that keep piling up unnecessarily in the corner of the room. Nobody is going to read them again, so why are they there?

### WORN-OUT ACCESSORIES

This means belts, scarves and jewellery that may be from the older you but are now out of date and dowdy. Again, these items may have looked fantastic ten years ago, but let's be real and admit that belt you loved for many years is never going to fit around your waist again! I have always had a great love of bling jewellery but when I discovered I had too many boxes of it, I realised they had to find another home. Not knowing what to do with them, my mother suggested I put the bling around the Buddhas I have scattered around my home and garden. This was a great idea, so now all of my Buddhas and angels have lovely little necklaces around their heads and necks.

### OLD FURNITURE

Do you have an old chair that is falling to pieces and will surely kill someone if they sit on it? Please don't tell me it is worth a lot of money and you are going to sell it one day. Sell it today or get rid of it.

### UNINSPIRING ART

Have you checked out your home or office lately and had a second look at your paintings and posters on the wall? I would not be surprised if you no longer find them inspiring. Wall art can reflect how you see yourself in the world so they need to be inspiring. If you don't want to update your collection, try hanging what you do have in different locations.

## FRAYED OLD LINEN

I don't know how many times I have cleaned out my linen press and still had too many things that I don't need. How many towels do you need in a lifetime, and as for sheets, if they are discoloured and old, why not throw them out? Perhaps you can give them to someone if they are still quite new. Remember, everything has a use-by date, and always remember to get rid of old frayed towels, washers with holes, and sheets you no longer need or are ever going to use.

## BROKEN KITCHEN UTENSILS

Make sure that your oven and all appliances are clean, up-to-date, and functional, and watch out for gas leaks, broken electricals, and never leave dirty plates lying on the sink for days. Check your kitchenware too. Old blackened pots, pans, plastic containers without the tops, old tins, glass jars, chipped cups, and cracked glasses can go. Old, broken or worn knives, forks, spoons, and let's not forget the chipped dishes you want to keep as they were a present from your grandmother — make sure you throw them out, as you don't need them for a rainy day. Always check there are no sharp knives on display as this is bad feng shui, and for good luck, I always have a large yellow chicken in my kitchen.

## OUT OF DATE FOOD

Always check the use-by dates and throw out anything that's past its time. If you have jars with a small amount of food left in the bottom that you know won't be used, put it in the bin.

## PAINT TINS AND OLD TOOLS

Old paint tins that just keep sitting there, year after year in some cupboard, need to go. Let's face it, you are never going to use them so it is always best, instead of storing them away for a rainy day, to take them straight to the dump as they can be toxic. It is not a good thing if they fall off the shelf and onto your head! There are special disposal methods that your local council may want you to follow if the paint is toxic, so do us all a favour and look it up.

## OLD TOYS AND TRINKETS

These precious things are just items you have collected and are never going to be used. Some old trinkets can also hold energy that may not be in your best interests. Erica was a lovely German lady I used to know and her hobby was to make and collect beautiful antique dolls. They used to smile at you very sweetly, with angelic little painted faces.

Every time I went to her place she would take them out and show me what she had made for them, and then she would put them very carefully back into the glass cupboards so they would not collect dust. On the weekend she was often off to fairs and doll workshops. This was a wonderful hobby that she had for many years until she developed arthritis in her hands and was no longer able to sew beautiful dresses for her much loved dolls. When she died I was given several of the dolls and had them displayed in my spare bedroom window.

Everything went well until my sister slept over one fateful night with her three naughty children. All hell broke loose when one of the boys claimed that the dolls talked to him all night, and he even went so far as to say that one of them, a funny clown on a hanging string, tried to strangle him. I just put it down to the incredible imagination of the kids. Not long after, I packed up the dolls and took them down to my mother's house thinking that she would love them. A week later my mother rang me and said in a stern voice that she demanded I come and pick them up as they were creepy and she could hear noises all the time from the room where they were stored.

Thinking how the whole thing was totally ridiculous, I packed them up and sure enough, *I* freaked out this time, because every time I walked into the room where I proudly displayed my dolls, I could have sworn that ten pairs of tiny little cold glass eyes were intensely watching me. Not long after, I told my husband the ridiculous story as I could not shake off the awful feeling I had. As soon as he heard what happened, he told me in no uncertain terms that they had to go. The church across the road was thrilled to receive the generous gift and I am sure they all sold at the local fete.

## PLASTIC, FAKE OR DEAD PLANTS

If there is one thing I don't tolerate when clearing a space, it is dead or fake plants. Not only are fake plants ugly, drab, and sad, they look shabby. They do not have good chi energy and are often full of dirt and dust. There is nothing more inspiring and better for the senses than to walk into a home and see a beautiful bouquet of fresh and sweet smelling flowers, standing in a vase full of fresh, clean water, waiting to greet you. Healthy green plants also bring in good chi energy for the inhabitants living in your home.

## HOUSEHOLD REPAIRS

Never ignore or leave house repairs, and always fix leaking taps, blocked drains, and blown light bulbs. In feng shui, leaking taps represent leaking money and no one wants that. Other broken things around the home can cause problems in your life too. These sound like simple things but they can cause unnecessary leaks and blocks of energy.

# CHAPTER TWO

## *Unwanted Spirits in Your Home*

Sometimes you may have more than just simple clutter in your home. Occasionally, a lost soul is found lurking in a home causing all types of havoc. On more than one occasion I have been called to a house that needed more than just a simple cleanse or feng shui. Part of my life's work as a psychic medium is releasing earthbound spirits. Earthbound spirits are not able or don't want to pass over.

There are a number of reasons this may happen. The death may have been accidental, they don't want to leave, or there is a fear of crossing over. Sometimes, religious beliefs may hold someone back if they have done something bad and therefore think they are going to hell. Other factors could also be obsessive love, greed for the material world, and attachment to earthly possessions.

Earthbound spirits generally congregate around large groups of people at places like hospitals, railways, shopping centres, airports, schools, or homes where they once lived. They are rarely found in a lonely old home, like what we see in movies, as they need lots of energy to stay earthbound. If you have a lost soul or earthbound spirit in your home, it will not go unnoticed as you will have quite a few issues. Here are some of the problems you may encounter.

1) Your home will feel ice-cold and downright unpleasant in certain areas, and no matter what you do, the energy will be heavy and unbearable to live in.
2) Most of the family living there will feel tired, have colds, or unexplained illness. They will also feel stuck in their lives.
3) There may be continual fights, arguments, or disagreements because of the imbalance of the energy in the house.
4) It will be impossible to sell or make changes to the house because of constant, unexplained delays.
5) You may have unexplained or continual problems with electricity or water for reasons that aren't obvious.
6) There may be unusual sounds, knocks, things disappearing, strange smells, or constant confusion.

## CLEANSING EARTHBOUND SPIRITS

If you have at least two of the above problems, it is more than likely you will have a lost spirit or ghost in your home. In most cases, it is generally more terrified of you than the other way around. Once the earthbound spirit or spirits are removed and sent into a *vortex*, or porthole of light, the energy in the space will no longer feel toxic, uncomfortable, cold or unpleasant, and the space will generally go back to normal. The space will no longer feel *heavy* and everything will feel lighter once again. The other good thing is life will once again return to normal and things will start to flow.

Earthbound spirits survive on living energy. Smudging and dried gum leaves are like fly spray for these spirits.

*Smudging* is a spiritual process and an ancient custom used by shamans and indigenous people in certain parts of the world. It involves clearing any negative or stuck energy in the home by giving it a good sage smudge or smoking. What you need to do is mix some dried sage and dried gum leaves together in a pot and then burn the mix, allowing the strong pungent smoke to clear any negative energy in your space. Walk through every room, allowing the smoke to weave through the space.

A few years ago, I was clearing a space in the bush, but could not get rid of the Aboriginal spirits that I sensed were around. After connecting with a good friend who was indigenous, it was suggested to use gum leaves and call in the spirit elder from the tribe of the soul who was stuck. We asked him for permission to send those spirits into the light that were dead, but stuck in limbo. My friend had a lot of experience as all this information was passed down when she was a small child. No sooner had I done this, I saw a spirit dressed in what appeared to be tribal gear suddenly leave and fly out the window. It was amazing how much lighter the energy felt when everything settled down.

Once any negative or heavy energy leaves, your space will feel lighter which will allow for good chi energy to return. Some people like to use a bell after they cleanse to welcome the positive energy back.

Many people are affected by negative energy in their home, space, or workplace as negative energy can drain your vitality, leaving you depressed, amongst other things. Sometimes, if left for long periods, it can make you feel quite ill, and stop good things coming to you in your life.

If you have cleared your space and are still having problems, you need to call in professionals, like a medium who is trained in this department. If a spirit has a strong connection to the house and they will not go, consider asking a medium to help release them.

To find a medium, you simply have to ask by word of mouth. You can also try the internet or get in contact with your local spiritual church. The work of a medium is always very draining as we work between two worlds. I always take another person with me, preferably a dowser who can work with earth energies, and after I have talked to the spirit or spirits stuck in the astral plane and helped crossed them over, the dowser will usually help me clear what we call *fractured energy*, or altered states of energy, to help bring harmony and balance back to the home once again. After I have finished clearing the space, I will also suggest ways to feng shui the home to bring more balance, harmony, and peace back into the space.

## VISITING LIVING SPIRITS

Living spirits are the majority of spirits that have crossed over successfully into the light or have 'gone home' to the spirit world. These are not a problem. Often, they are family members or loved ones in the *spirit world*, which is an arm's length away in another dimension, trying to make a connection of love to let us know that they are still with us, and watching what we do in our daily lives.

When we cross over as souls into the spirit world, we return to our spirit home and cluster groups. We are always with our guide, angel or a loved one. It is a time of transition and of great celebration within the spirit world. Once there, we are taken by our guide to our own soul groups, and we are given a *life review* by advanced spirit elders. We discuss our life on earth, how we understood the lessons, and receive healing in the place of *Oneness,* which is often described as the *spirit hospital.* The place of Oneness can only be described as all-consuming and incredibly full of unconditional love.

From my own near-death experience when I was younger, I can honestly say that the spirit world is an incredible and vast consciousness of light and love and healing. It is also, according to my guide and my own experience from past life regression, a recycling place for reincarnation. Some people refer to the afterlife as heaven and indeed, so too do many loved ones and spirits I have spoken to with clients. They will often say that it is similar to earth, that you don't need food, and it is a beautiful place which is a lot brighter; not as heavy and dense as earth, and where everyone looks younger as there is no disease.

# CHAPTER 3

## Cures For Enhancing Positive Energy

Once you've cleared negative and toxic energies, or unwanted spirits from your home, you can now use special *cures* that are meant to inspire, create, and encourage positive experience in your life. When working with feng shui, it's important to use cures that resonate with you. These simple remedies can improve your life as they attract positive energy into your space or home. But whatever you do, don't use too many cures otherwise you may create clutter and blockages again. It is a matter of deciding what feels right for you to bring harmony and peace into your home. As you begin to play with the energy, your home will begin to speak to you and you will be amazed at what it will say.

The first step to working with feng shui is to buy a compass and learn how to use it. You can buy a regular compass from a camping shop, and often, they come with instructions. Next you need the basic floor plan of your house. You may have a plan from the real estate agent when you purchased or rented your home, otherwise you will need to draw it up yourself.

Once you have the floor plan, mark the *north, south, east,* and *west* corners. After that, mark the *north-east, south-east, north-west,* and *south-west.*

Next, mark each direction in your main living room. The living room is a very important room for feng shui — not only because it's central to family life — it's also the one room that can affect the entire house, boost cures, and minimise afflictions.

## IN WITH THE NEW

Buy a new plant and put it in the *east* corner of your living room to symbolise a new beginning. Stock your fridge and pantry with food, and make the beds with clean, fresh sheets. Open all your windows to bring in fresh air, and to allow in the *new.*

## CRYSTALS

Crystals, besides having their own properties, are natural conduits of energy. Once you have attuned and programmed them to what you need or want in a certain area of your home, they will attract and draw the type of positive energy that you asked for in order to create a wonderful environment in which to relax and recharge. Quartz crystals, for example, can be programmed to draw in light energy which can shield you, your loved ones, and your space from unwanted negative energy or unwanted outside forces.

Crystals are best placed in the Earth and Metal element directions, the *south-west, centre, west, north-west* or *north-east* corner of your home or room.

To program your crystal, hold it in your left hand very firmly, and ask it to give you all its powers. Once you have done this you will feel a tingling feeling in your hand or arm. You then hold it in your right hand and command it to do what you want, for example, "*I now ask the crystal to attract good energy for abundance in life.*" Another example is to ask the crystal for extra protection for your family.

Cleansing your crystals of negative energy is also important for creating good energy in your home because they are natural absorbers of etheric or auric energies. You can cleanse them by many methods such as placing them under a full moon in a bowl of water and sea salt, or soaking them gently in a bath with lavender oil. Whenever I soak my crystals, I like to give them at least 48 hours as I imagine them singing with appreciation like small children as they soak in the beautiful oils and water of the bath. You may even choose to bury your crystals in the earth for several days with the pointed section facing up, and if placed in the earth with a plant, it will always help the sick plant flourish as it is said that crystals have healing modalities and love to be back in the cool earth with a plant for company.

The proof is always in the pudding though, so why not give it a try if you have green fingers? A point to remember though; never place your crystal in a strong sun, especially in the middle of the day, as they will fade and lose their colours.

My front door is north-east facing, so I've placed a clear quartz crystal on the hallstand, and have programmed it to bring more abundance into my life. On my desk I always have a beautiful amethyst, as this is an excellent choice for nervous tension, or for people who may worry or stress when it comes to keeping up with deadlines. A large amethyst stone is a very practical stone as it helps ground your energies when placed at your feet.

There are so many crystals to work with, so it is up to you to decide what attracts you the most as it is entirely a personal thing. Here are some of my favourite crystals. You might choose to employ them when you have cleared your home.

Apophyllite is a beautiful crystal, a brilliant green in colour. It is an uplifting stone and is very good for clearing the energy centres in the body, or *chakras*. It is good for opening the crown chakra, bringing in creative ideas to help with your work, and especially good for writers or energy workers. I have one on my desk for when I see clients.

Aquamarine is a pale blue colour and is very good for communication. It works on the throat chakra and connects to our thoughts and emotions. When placed in the *helpful people* section of the home, *relationship* section and *career* section, it will enhance positive communication.

Citrine is generally yellow or brown, and is used to bring more money into your life. You can have it on your desk, when using your map of Bagua, in your *career* section, *abundance* section or *fame* section of the home.

Hematite is a bold crystal that has a silvery polish to it. It is very grounding and good to carry in your pocket. It brings out inner strength. I love having this stone in the family room or kitchen of the home.

Lapis Lazuli is a deep blue crystal with tiny flecks of gold throughout. This has to be my favourite as it is a good crystal to enhance your intuitive abilities. It is also an excellent stone for meditation. I often wear this stone as a necklace as I love its properties. This would be a good stone to have in every area of your home, especially the bedroom, where you sleep and rest, to help enhance positivity, clear chi, and help your intuition.

Rose quartz is a pink crystal, and is what I call the love crystal. I always recommend this crystal for use in children's bedrooms as the crystal has a playful energy, yet is very healing and calming. Children naturally resonate with the energy of this crystal. It is also a great stone to have on your desk and in your jewellery as its properties are very calming. Place a rose quartz in the *relationship* section of your home.

Smokey quartz comes in a range of different sizes, and is brown to black. This is a good stone for psychic protection as it dissolves negative energy and emotional blockages. It is also a grounding stone and can help with concentration. This is a great stone to place in the *career* section of your home, the *fame* section of your home, and in bedrooms.

Turquoise is a light blue opaque stone. It amplifies healing energy, and strengthens and focuses mental communication. It is a great stone to wear for general health and is great for the bedrooms.

Obsidian is black volcanic glass. It is a powerful crystal as its energy cuts through conscious thought patterns revealing whatever lies beneath. It is also a great grounding stone for people that suffer from a lack of concentration, and is good for psychic protection as it acts as a barrier. This stone is also very useful for breaking down old conditioned patterns which restrict us, and is usually good for people that may feel stuck in their life or work, as its properties offer clarity for the mind. This is great for your bedrooms, and good for the *relationship* section of the home.

Sapphire, as a mineral, varies in colour but is most commonly blue or red. This crystal is known as the crystal of prosperity as it is said to fulfill the dreams and desires of the consciousness. This mineral can also get rid of unwanted thoughts and bring joy and peace to the mind, opening it up to beauty and intuition. This is a great crystal to have in the *career* section of the home, and the *wealth* section.

Malachite is a popular green crystal which is worn mostly as jewellery. Its qualities are unique as it is good for suppressed emotions, particularly those related to areas where we limit our powers. I love having this crystal in the *relationship* section of the home.

Quartz crystals are large crystals that are conduits of energy, and can be attuned to whatever you want or need. They vary in size, shape, and colour but are very effective and powerful for manifesting what you need in your life. These can be placed anywhere in the home.

## MIRRORS

Mirrors are a wonderful addition to homes as they bring light to dark areas and help redirect energy. Light dispels negative energy. If you are feeling stuck in your life or if you live in a dark home with little light, a mirror can be very beneficial.

There are a few feng shui rules when it comes to mirror placement. The most important rule is that your mirror doesn't reflect something unpleasant like a bathroom. You want your mirror to reflect a beautiful view like a garden or the sky. A mirror facing the dining table is also thought to be beneficial as it magnifies abundance. If you have a really small room, a mirror can open up the space. A mirror is also good in a long hallway as it can slow down the flow of chi.

There are places in your home that don't do well with a mirror. Mirrors in bedrooms that reflect the bed are considered taboo in feng shui because they can be over-stimulating and encourage insomnia. It's also not a good idea to place a mirror opposite a front door. This can reflect incoming energy right back out the door, so if you want a mirror in your entry, you can place it on a side wall, just not facing the front door.

## SOUNDS AND SMELLS

Throughout my home and garden I have different types of wind chimes and little tinkling bells that sound beautifully relaxing when a gentle breeze is blowing. The beautiful sounds bring pleasure to the senses and are a gentle reminder of the importance of my own inner peace and tranquility in my private surroundings for my family, my welcomed visitors, and myself in my little world.

The energy the sound creates is very healing and relaxing, and creates a sense of inner peace and harmony for all. Every time the wind hits them it creates a healing wave of positive sounds which wash over the home, bringing pleasure to the senses.

Wind chimes can be used suppress or remove negative energy in the home, so they work to both cure and energise. The key to getting wind chimes to work in your home is to choose the right material and the right location.

If you want to enhance the energy of your home; ceramic and glass wind chimes are best place in the *north-east* or *south-west*.

Wood or bamboo wind chimes can be placed in the *east, south-east,* and *south.* Metal wind chimes are best placed in the *north, north-west,* and *west.*

If you want use a wind chime to cure a problem area, such as the placement of a toilet, use a wood wind chime in the *south-west* or *north-east,* a metal wind chime in the *east* or *south-east,* or a glass wind chime in the *north.*

If you want to enhance the energy in an area use hollow rod chimes, and if you are trying to suppress negative energy, use solid rod chimes.

Another important aspect to your home is to always pay attention to smells. Fresh air is the best, so always remember to open your doors and windows and have fresh air circulating at all times for a healthier way of living. Another way of improving the energy in your home is to use essential oils or pleasant smelling incense which can create a calming effect. Therapeutic oils are very healing and have qualities to help with relaxation. Orange and lemon essentials oils are very uplifting, lavender is calming, and eucalyptus oil can help clean the air.

## PLANTS AND WATER

Throughout my home I have an abundance of plants, fish, and flowers. I will also make sure that I have a vase of fresh flowers as it makes me feel good, and I love the smell of their fresh perfume in my home. This is optional, of course, and is entirely up to you and where your tastes lie.

I always make a point of changing the water every day, as water is a natural conduit of energy and helps absorb negative energy from the atmosphere in the home. Beautiful, colourful flowers are great to have around the home and the same goes for soft, leafy green plants and succulents, as they are natural gifts from the elemental kingdom in nature and spirit.

Fake flowers are fine so long as they do not collect dust, are kept clean, and look good. It is all about what feels right. I always love to have soft, healthy plants in the living areas, however, I advise people to avoid plants and flowers in the bedroom.

Another good way to get energy moving is to have mobiles and fountains in your home, particularly in the *north*. Keep water features out of your bedroom though. If your bedroom is in located in the *north*, add a water feature to the *north* corner of your living room. In my *fame* and *career* section of my home, I have a water fountain. This has helped my career immensely because they are a symbol of the constantly moving chi energy in these sections of my home. The sound and sight of water fountains are also lovely to have in the house. I find the constant, rhythmical sound of running water to be very calming.

A warning though, be very careful with water features as they are intangible energies that create amplifications of the energy present, regardless of whether its positive or negative. For people who are not having a feng shui consultation, I would advise that you test the placement of the water feature first. Pay attention to the flow of chi, of energy, and assess what happens after a few months.

As an additional note, I also have birdbaths in my front yard to encourage birds. When you have birds around, you will always have a happy house and happy life.

## BEAUTIFUL OBJECTS

I am a great collector of stones, shells and crystals. I have many of these beautiful items that I have collected from all over the world, giving me fond memories of my travels in life, as I totally love anything to do with nature. To me, they are priceless pieces of art and are scattered throughout my home. I also have a large, smiling Buddha at the front door which represents peace and protection in my meditation room and office. This is also a symbol to attract positive and universal peace energy into my space. I also have statues of angels. Angels have been known throughout time to be the harbingers of peace and harmony on earth. This reminds me that we are never alone. In times of great upheaval, these amazing spirit beings can be called on at any time to help us in our daily lives, or help us when in trouble.

## MUSIC

It is always good to have music in your home as it creates an amazing ambience, and music is not only fun, but inspirational for the soul. You don't have to be a musical genius to have instruments in your home, but just having them around can be inspirational as they can be used for play. In a busy world, we sometimes forget to enjoy ourselves and music, no matter how it is used, is always a good thing as it is relaxing and can create positive chi energy in the background. The sound of music is often very healing as it can be heartfelt, creative, and gives us a sense of freedom in a sometimes very dark and troubled world. Music is food for the soul. Throughout my journey in life, I have amassed a large collection of musical instruments which I have learnt to play. When friends come over, it is a great way to relax and have a bit of fun. I also have many drums which everyone, no matter their talent, can play, so it is always good to play along with friends who come to visit.

Crystal bowls are also very special for creating music in the home. They work on a vibrational level when played and can clear out negative energy in a home, office, or from the chakra system in the human body. Playing crystal bowls helps to create a lighter, calmer, and clearer energy in the home.

I often use crystal bowls at the end of my spirit shows, along with drumming, to clear out blocked energy from people in the audience that may have been processing emotional issues before and during my show, or at the end of the healing sessions that I run. This generally makes them feel energised, centred, and relaxed.

## ELEMENTS, ENERGY, AND COLOURS

Often, numbers and colours, along with elements, will play an important part in changing your luck or good fortune as they are renowned to have hidden qualities or influential powers. For example, I have always loved the number six as I feel that it is auspicious and has brought me luck throughout my life. To me, the house number six, single or when you add up the digits, means stability, and is excellent for creative and artistic people like myself. It is said that when you live in a house numbered six your life will improve out of sight.

My recommendation is to have the same wall colour throughout the whole house to keep the balance. You can bring in additional colours with furnishings. In feng shui, it is recommended that you align your colour selections with the elements.

The element of the *north* is Water, and colours including *black*, *blue*, and *purple* are good for rooms in the north sector of your home. Black represents accumulated wealth and financial opportunities. Blue represents generating wealth and is useful for growth, both spiritual and financial. Purple is an important colour in feng shui and can be used in any room of the house, but is particularly good in the north sector as it enhances opportunity and confidence. Water is enhanced by Metal, so you can also have Metal colours in the north sector of the home. If you have a problem area, like a toilet in the north sector, you need to exhaust or destroy the energy associated with the problem. Water is destroyed by Wood and Earth elements, so only use these colours in the north sector of the home if you want to fix a problem.

The element of the *south* is Fire, and colours including *red* and *pink* are good for rooms in the south sector of your home. Red is another important colour in feng shui as it is said to stimulate chi, passion, and abundance. Pink represents love, joy, and friendship. The Fire element is enhanced by Wood, exhausted by Earth and destroyed by Water.

The element of the *north-east*, *centre*, and *south-west* is Earth, with colours including *tan*, *beige*, and *yellow* good for rooms in these sectors. Earth is enhanced by Fire, so you can have those colours in this sector too. The Earth element is destroyed by Wood and exhausted by Metal. Yellow is considered the colour of power, energy, and intellect in feng shui. It's a great colour for someone who needs grounding.

The element of the *east* and *south-east* is Wood. The colours of *green* and *brown* are good for rooms in these sectors. Wood is enhanced by Water, so you can also have these colours in this sector too. The Wood element is destroyed by Metal and exhausted by Fire. The colour green signifies growth and harmony in feng shui. It is also a healing and calming colour, and can be used to bring new opportunities into your life. Brown represents stability.

The element of the *west* and *north-west* is Metal, with colours including *grey*, *white*, and *gold* good for this sector. The Metal element is enhanced by Earth so you can have these colours here too. Metal is destroyed by Fire and exhausted by Water. Grey is a good colour for problem-solving, gold promotes wisdom, and white aids mental clarity, fresh beginnings and resolved endings.

## HOUSE NUMBERS

In feng shui, there is a belief that every home has its own spirit and energy. This concept is an aspect and not a principal, but it is believed that certain numbers can aid you by attracting specific energies into your life, and some numbers can even bring good fortune to you.

Numbers, in most cultures, play a significant role. In many cultures, the number 13 is believed to be an unlucky number, but if you add it up and take it to the next level in numerology, so 1+3=4, it also becomes an inauspicious number in Cantonese as it sounds like the word for death. It is not looked upon as favorable by the Chinese in real estate, in particular. In certain cultures, your house number alone can determine your home's resale value. To neutralise the negative effects of all dreaded numbers, all you have to do is encircle the number in the signage and all negative effects will disappear. You will be able to move into your new dwelling, confident that no negative energies will be drawn to your home.

What does your house number say about you? If you have a house number with multiple digits, add each number separately until you come back to a single number. For example, number 149 would be 1+4+9=14, and then 1+4=5.

1. This is a number of responsibility and independence. The number one can also promote loneliness so make sure you have a good job or plenty of things and hobbies to do. If you are looking for a long-term partner or a nurturing family life, the number one home may not be for you. This is a house number that is about individuality, ambition, and leadership.

2. This house is for busy people who often keep late nights, and are always coming and going. The number two home is a place where love, family, and friends are high on the priority list, so if you are looking for a place to nest this is it. This number also attracts psychic people and those that are sensitive to energy. The number two also attracts people that are community minded, into welfare, and caring.

3. This is a good energy for people that love travel, enjoy adventure, and like to be in the limelight. Not for the faint-hearted, this home is for ambitious, successful people that like to give life a go, are adventurous, and like to take risks. Sometimes, people in this house can have money problems as they like to live large. If you want a quiet life, the number three home is not for you, however, if you are creative and like socialising, the number three home is great.

4. This address has a very challenging energy and can be unpredictable. Some people believe that living in a number four home may be unlucky. A remedy for this is to just to go with the flow. The number four home also requires slow and

steady work to build stability. This house will support growing a family, business, and wealth if you are willing to plan strategically and put the work in. A garden is a good representation for the number four home. You can start with a dirt patch and a few seeds but with time, patience, and work you can create a thriving masterpiece.

5. This is a great number for running a business from home, as it is a high energy environment with many things going on all the time for the occupants. If you are planning on having a quiet family life, this is not the right number for you as this number energy always attracts people that like to be busy and travel. This home is often a good investment. While fun and freedom is the theme for the number five home, be wary of excess and overindulgence.

6. This is a good and favourite number for families, and a home for stability as people tend to be here with this number for a long time. This energy usually attracts people that are artistic or talented, and tends to draw the better qualities out of anyone who lives here, especially if they have a creative nature. This is a harmonious home and good for romance. While this is a nurturing home, it can bring out perfectionist tendencies so don't forget to look after yourself as well as tend to your family.

7. This is home that is renowned for problems with plumbing and structure. The number seven home is also a place for introspection, learning, and contemplation. It can be a place to develop your spirituality and intuition, rather than material gains. If your priority is building a high-energy career, this may not be the best home for you. However, if you are a writer, or work in a specialised area, a number seven home can be

great for you as it supports intellectual pursuits. Relationships and marriages also require extra effort in a number seven home because the energy is more internally focused. It is also a number that holds memories and is sensitive to energies, so people that are highly sensitive need to be careful of their health. A number seven home is also not advised for people who struggle with drug or alcohol issues.

8. This is a home that is perfect for older people, or younger people that are mature, and promotes abundance in all areas of life. This is also a great home for getting ahead in the material world. Opportunities are high for people in a number eight home who want to make the most of their natural gifts or talents. However, people living in a number eight home need to make sure that making money doesn't become their only priority and that they continue to connect and give back to their family and the community.

9. Be careful with this home as sometimes it can attract problems with neighbours. Zodiac signs like Aries and Scorpio will be attracted to this number as it will help them advance with their careers. Travel is indicated as well for the occupants of this home, along with books and literature. This number will also bring out your natural hidden talents, but a number nine home can indicate accidents, so be careful. The number nine home promotes creativity, spirituality, and forgiveness. It can also help you to develop your intuition.

## FRONT DOOR

The front door is very important in feng shui. It is called the *mouth of the house*, and is predominantly where energy enters your home. To bring more abundance into my home, I painted my front door a lovely shade of maroon red. Within weeks of doing this, my husband's career went through the roof and my own business expanded as well. I would never have believed it if I hadn't tried it for myself, but that is how feng shui works.

It's important that you actively use your front door to improve the energy of your home, and to keep it well-maintained. If it has peeling paint or squeaky hinges, it is time for an overhaul.

Select the colour of your door based on the direction that it faces. If you are standing inside looking out, the direction you are facing is the direction of your front door.

Houses faces *north-east, south-west,* and *south* work well with a *red* front door.

Houses facing *north, east,* and *south-east* work well with a *blue, black,* or *purple* front door.

House facing *west* and *north-west* work well with a *white* or *grey* front door.

Houses facing *south, east,* and *south-east* work well with a *wooden* front door.

I also have a wind chime by the door outside to lift energy, and a few happy Buddhas to greet guests. Placing potted plants on either side of the front door helps to draw more energy into the home. I've got two big and healthy succulent plants flanking the front door to boost chi.

## TAKING CARE OF YOU

You can have the best cures around your home and work environment, but if you don't take care of your own wellbeing then they are a complete waste of time. Working with respect and care towards your own energy is just as important as working with the energy around you.

## DIET

Make sure you eat a balanced diet to ensure your body has the fuel it needs to do the things you want. Moderation is key, and that includes alcohol.

## BATH

When you are feeling drained of energy, have a good soak for at least twenty minutes in a warm bath with either a handful of Epsom salts or sea salt. Many people love to bathe with all types of special oils like lavender, or rose oil even, as it is so relaxing, but I prefer natural ingredients myself. This will clear away any negative energy and debris that you may have collected in your aura or energy field, making you feel very relaxed and pampered. Waving a smoking sage stick through your aura will do the same, as will Australian dried gum leaves. Indigenous people have used this technique for years in ceremonies and healing work.

## CLOAKING

If you want to protect yourself in a particular environment, or if you do not want to be noticed when you are walking into a room, or even when you are out and about, pull your aura in and imagine you are wearing an invisible cloak of white. Then, wrap a layer of blue around you. This will pull in your energy, and you will be able to walk around and mix with people without them paying you too much attention.

## MUSIC

Putting on music, drumming, or playing an instrument can be very uplifting for the spirit. It opens the heart chakra and allows love into your body, mind and cells.

## MEDITATION

Meditating for at least twenty minutes a day and making positive affirmations are an energy boost. Make it a rule to close down all of your chakras or energy points after you work with people or meditate. This is a good way to protect yourself so you are not open to be affected by other people's energy or vibrations.

## CREATE AN ALTAR FOR MANIFESTATION

Whenever I want to manifest my desires, I create what I fondly call an *altar*, a place where I can call for happiness, healing, success, love, and the desires which are always in alignment with my highest good. By focusing on your power to manifest a prosperous life, you are opening up the universal flow to you and the people around you.

To create an altar, find a small table and cover it with a clean white cloth. On the table you are creating an energy grid of prayer, to manifest your desires.

Place three large white candles in a glass container in the middle of the table, with the name and picture of the prosperity goddesses on each one.

The first candle is represented by *Lakshmi*, the beautiful Hindu goddess of prosperity that works very closely with Ganesh, the Hindu elephant-headed deity that overcomes obstacles.

*Fortuna,* the Greek Goddess of fortune, goes on the second candle. *Abundantia,* the Roman Goddess of plenty, is the third who can bring you opportunities and success.

On the outer side of these three candles, place a large white candle for the Christ's consciousness energy of unconditional love, and a large green candle to burn off any jealousy and envy that may be projected your way.

Make sure you also add some fresh flowers to invoke the calming energy of the nature spirits, a few crystals of choice (for instance rose quartz and lapis lazuli), and symbols of the four archangels.

I also like to work with the goddess *Isis* for strength and power, and *Mother Mary* for healing and miracles.

Once you have done all this, place a small red candle for each wish you want in your life. You can also place a small picture of yourself with a loved one, or by yourself in a red frame to improve loving relationships in your life.

When you are ready to use your sacred altar, all you have to do is light all the candles, make all your wishes, and do a small meditation with prayers to the divine spirit. This should be a daily thing.

Make sure that when you are finished, you blow out all the candles.

Now sit back and watch the universe create miracles for you.

## STAY GROUNDED

Grounding exercises such as walking, martial arts, going to the gym, dancing, or doing yoga help raise your energy and will prevent you from feeling depleted. Exercise, a healthy diet, and taking care of yourself will keep you grounded. A lot of students I have worked with over the years have had this problem. When they are not grounded to the earth, they are very scattered and not able to grow spiritually and reach their higher powers.

## FUN

Make time for fun with friends and loved ones. I don't know how many times I tell myself this, and all my friends and clients. This is something that we always forget to do. Having a good laugh and catching up with friends is good for the soul, and lifts your vibration so you can create the world that you want to live in.

## HEALTHY BOUNDARIES

Have healthy boundaries. Don't feel depleted by too many people, family or friends continually taking your energy. Set goals and see how fast you can manifest them. Often, it is a smart move to sit back and let people and loved ones work out their own problems. It is all about personal responsibility, and allowing them to sort out their own issues is more empowering for them as souls.

## NEGATIVITY

Get rid of people that are draining and negative. You will find they are just sucking your energy and wasting your time. I can't stress enough how important this is. You need to have supportive friends, not just people that you feel you need to help all the time.

## LEARN TO SAY THE MAGIC WORD — NO!

Learn to say NO. It feels good and is so powerful. Take your power back! Boundaries are a healthy practice to have. It is a difficult thing to do in the beginning, especially with all the *poor me* talk in the world, but once you get going, you won't look back. Look out world, here you come!

## CLUTTER

Lose the clutter. Get rid of anything that does not serve you as it is just blocking your energy. That, of course, can mean people as well.

## SELF LOVE AND FORGIVENESS

Most importantly, learn to love yourself. If you don't, nobody else will. Be willing to forgive loved ones, people, or friends who have hurt you in some way. This can be really hard as these painful lessons can take you off your path, disempower you, and hold you back from where you are meant to be. It may be sad in some cases, especially if you don't have these people in your life again, but if they are meant to come back, and have the right energy for you, they will return when their own lessons are complete.

An easy way to work at forgiveness is to place a person in a large pink healing bubble of love, tell them that you forgive them, and let them go. Surrender your pain to the spirit world.

# CHAPTER 4

# *The Bagua*

Once you have cleared the clutter from your space or home, it is time to use the Bagua.

The Bagua acts as a map for your home or space, so you can access deeper information about all areas of your life. The Bagua (pronounced *ba-gwa*), is a chart, map, or blueprint feng shui analysts use when working with changing energy in the home as it represents a specific life situation that addresses the energy in that particular section. It is like a horoscope in a way. It's made up of eight sections with the ninth element in the centre, which is displayed as a yin yang symbol of balance, and is referred to as the tai chi. Its divisions of heaven and earth, mountain and lake, fire and water, thunder and wind, represent virtually every aspect of life.

When you begin to work with the Bagua, align the map to the main entrance of your office, home, place of work, desk, or the front door. Do this by standing in the doorway with your back to the street, and from there, you can begin to identify and locate the sections of your home on the map of the Bagua.

For example, if your home is like a square, and the front door is in the middle, then you are in the *career* section of your home, the *relationship* section is the far right corner of the home, and the *wealth* section is far left section of the home.

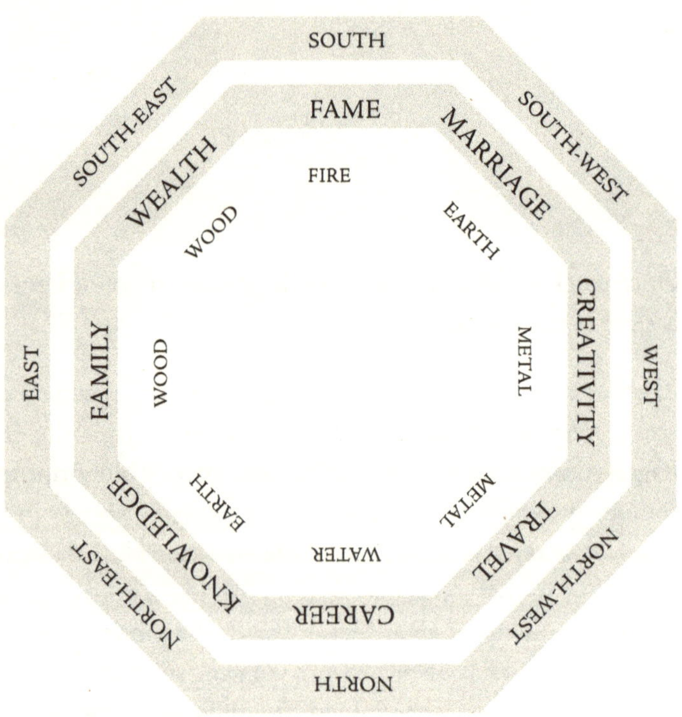


**The main tools used in feng shui analysis are the compass and the Bagua map.**

THE SUMMARY OF DIRECTIONS

NORTH – Career

Your sense of self-worth or self-esteem.

**NORTH-EAST – Inner Knowledge/Wisdom**

How well you see yourself in the world and your wisdom.

**EAST – Family, Ancestors, Friendships, and Health**

The support you need with family, friendships, and the health section.

**SOUTH-EAST – Wealth and Prosperity**

The law of attraction, abundance, and prosperity.

**SOUTH – The Fame and Reputation**

Being recognised for all your accomplishments in life.

**SOUTH-WEST – Relationship and Marriage**

Love, romance, and everyday relationships in your life.

**WEST – Children, Creativity and Projects**

This means all aspects: physical, emotional, mental, and spiritual.

**NORTH-WEST – Helpful People/Travel**

Networking, connections, and influential people.

## THE CURES

When selecting cures, it's a good idea to work with the elements. So if your career and front door is in the *north*, introduce Water and Metal colours and objects, such as water features, shells, and fish (Water), metallic bowls and wind chimes (Metal).

For rooms in the *north-east, centre,* and *south-west,* introduce Earth and Fire colours and objects such as lamps, candles (Fire), pictures of landscapes, ceramics, and crystals (Earth).

For rooms in the *east* and *south-east* introduce Wood and Water objects like plants (Wood) or a fish tank (Water).

For rooms in the *west* and *north-west* introduce Metal and Earth objects.

For rooms in the *south* introduce Fire and Wood objects.

Look carefully in the room you are working with and place one or two objects if you feel that something is missing in the room. Whatever you do, don't use more than two to three cures, otherwise you will create clutter.

## MISSING SECTIONS

The square grid version of the Bagua is easier to use when dealing with missing sections.

You may experience sections or corners missing when you apply the Bagua. Although this can cause energetic imbalances, it can be easily fixed with a simple and easy cure. When I work as a consultant, I first work on the ground floor, then I will do the basement, and then upstairs until each floor is done. I apply the map for every room in every section. After I have finished, I will use my grid again and walk around the outside of the office or home, making adjustments to any blockages in energy with the shape of the premises, picking and using cures that I may come across as I work.

When you start to work with the cures and make adjustments in your home, you will find how easy it is, and how quickly it will work. You will improve your quality of life and it will be a better environment.

If you find working with the Bagua difficult, why not try and use the simple square version of the map?

| | | |
|---|---|---|
| Wealth | Fame | Relationships |
| Family<br>Health | Tai Chi | Creative<br>Children<br>Projects |
| Inner Knowledge<br>Intuition | Career | Helpful People<br>Travel |

| | | |
|---|---|---|
| Wealth | Fame | Relationships |
| Family<br>Health | Tai Chi | Creative<br>Children<br>Projects |
| Inner Knowledge<br>Intuition | | |

In this image, using the front door method with the Bagua map, the *career* and *helpful people/travel* sections are missing. This can be easily fixed on the outside of the home with cures to get the energy active.

An example of this was when I was called out to see a client that had set up a new business. Peter was a busy naturopath who had decided on a better life, so he moved his busy and successful practice to the country. After a couple months of not being able to make a proper living, he called me up and asked if I could give him any insights as he was feeling very despondent. He was starting to think that perhaps he had made a big mistake by moving from the city.

Once I arrived and had walked around the home, it was easy to see the problem as he had some sections missing from his home. I asked him to pick out some of my cures so he could get his business up and running.

After giving the house a good smoking and clearing with some white sage and gum leaves, we got rid of any negative past problems from the last tenants and then I suggested some cures like a wind chime, a birdbath, and some lovely green succulents to grow in attractive pots. I also suggested he paint his front door to his office a professional black. After all, it was not his home but his intended office.

After about six months, Peter emailed me and said his business had improved. He was experimenting and finding new cures as he found the whole subject fascinating. He could not believe how simple it was, and how it had worked to bring him life improvements.

| | | |
|---|---|---|
| | Fame | Relationships |
| Family<br>Health | Tai Chi | Creative<br>Children<br>Projects |
| Inner Knowledge<br>Intuition | Career | Helpful People<br>Travel |

The second diagram is an example of the *wealth* section missing. Believe it or not, this is very common in many houses. When I moved into my second house when our children were older, this whole section was missing on the outside of the home. Lucky for me, I knew how to rectify the problem.

In the missing wealth section, I cleared the clutter that was just laying around, like old brooms and pool equipment. I placed a gold Buddha with a shell necklace around its neck, hung a metal wind chime near the window, and placed a small colourful transfer of an angel of peace on the window. So far it has worked. I have always had no problems with finances and my world just gets better and better.

## CAREER SECTION

The *career* section is one of the main sections of your home to improve, especially if you want to excel, take charge of your life, and get to the top of your field in any chosen profession. You need to be inspired.

The career section is important because on another level, it indicates how you feel about yourself on a subconscious level. Keep this area clear of any clutter that may be blocking the entrance or space. This means going through drawers that may be full of old papers and stationery and throwing them out. You can then introduce one or two cures that enhance the direction of your home.

CASE STUDY: **Cassie**

Cassie was a very hard-working young woman but never seemed to get anywhere with her advertising job. No matter how hard she worked, she never seemed to get that promotion or step up like others that had been there longer than her. She was frustrated and extremely disappointed when she asked me to come and space clear her home.

When I walked in the front door of her home, I nearly fell over backwards. I was shocked to see that there was hardly any room to move as it was jam-packed full of old boxes that were filled with books and papers. Also, she had dozens of shoes (which did not seem to be taking her anywhere), that were scattered in piles in the small hallway, which not only belonged to her, but to her children and husband as well.

When I pointed this out to her she was embarrassed and said the family was always in a hurry, she so preferred to keep everyone's shoes near the door as it was easier when they had to go out. I suggested they must have a place, like in the owners rooms or in a cupboard, and to get rid of the shoes they never wore. I pointed out to Cassie that this was definitely half of her problem, as all clutter is toxic and blocks energy. It wasn't doing her any favours, especially as she was so frustrated in her work.

Happy to hear me out, I suggested that it would generate wonderful energy and be very auspicious to paint the front door red or green, which was the second choice for the outside, and to maybe think of placing three gold coins under the welcome mat in a red envelope. I asked her to think about buying a small water fountain to place on the sideboard instead of the boxes. For extra luck, I suggested that she buy a small green jade horse to face the front door so as to bring movement into the house.

Within three weeks of giving Cassie her instructions, my cures worked. She rang me up in excitement and said that she was up for promotion at work. Finally, I was sure that Cassie was on her way to a new and happier career.

### CASE STUDY: James

James was an accountant that had his own small business. No matter how hard he worked and tried to move ahead, he never seemed to get anywhere. Over time he became very disheartened.

His beautiful wife, who loved him very much, had an avid interest in feng shui and alternative therapies. She read an article I had written in a magazine about the power of positive energy, and was interested to see if I could help her husband in his work as he was becoming more and more depressed and disheartened. According to the wife, no matter how hard he worked, he never seemed to get ahead. It was like he was just plodding along.

On my arrival at the home, I noticed that the family lived in a cul-de-sac which is never a good thing in feng shui, so I gave her a few tips and remedies, like placing a small Bagua mirror (it's the same shape as the Bagua map, but has a mirror) out the front of the home to stop the neighbours energy coming in, and to also use a metal wind chime out the front of the home.

The other thing I noticed, and it stood out like a sore thumb too, was that her husband was a hoarder. There was so much clutter everywhere! It was in every nook and cranny of the house, and in a shed at the back of the property. When I pointed this out, the woman acknowledged this and said she had been on his back for ages, but would now take action herself and get rid of everything while he was at work, with the help of their children. The clutter was everywhere. It was piled up in mountains of junk, felt very unpleasant, and should have been discarded years before as there was hardly any room to walk around. It must have been unpleasant for everyone living in the house.

After I finished at the home, I was then asked to go to James's office, as both he and his wife were happy with my report. On arrival, I noticed that he worked with his back to the main entrance of his small office. Also, I could see how untidy and disorganised his office was with papers and important files everywhere. This was certainly very discouraging and I could not help but wonder how he managed to work efficiently at all, and was even able to think, with so much clutter and mess everywhere.

There was also poor ventilation in his office. I felt as if I could hardly breathe it was so stuffy, so I suggested to James that perhaps he should open a window sometimes to allow in fresh air. He agreed. He said that he suffered from allergies most of this life and always had a cold, so he thought it was better to keep the window closed, which was not good for him in the long term. When I told his wife this she laughed and agreed with everything I said. She disliked going to his office to visit him because it was always too stuffy and gave her a headache.

## INNER KNOWLEDGE/INTUITION SECTION

The *inner knowledge/self-worth/intuition* section is located in the *north-east* section of the home. This is a special part of your home as it holds the energy for inner knowledge, dreams, spirituality, and intuition, which is important for inner growth.

If this section is a bedroom, always open the blinds in the daytime to allow the light to come in and dispel any darkness. For inspiration, inner loving, and believing that your dreams can come true, think of hanging some calming or inspiring pictures on the wall — something that you can learn from. Another suggestion is to place a peaceful Buddha, or a statue of a lovely angel in the room, or maybe some beautiful rocks, or shells to display.

Activating this section of your home will attract people to you so you can gain information for positive self-worth to inspire you to live your dreams. I always love to have a pink salt lamp in this room to generate positive energy at all times. I only turn it off when I am away from the home for holidays or an extended period of time.

**CASE STUDY: Michael**

Michael was a sensitive, older man at a major turning point in his life. He was thinking of retiring but disliked being idle and had no idea what to do.

Throughout his life he had often dreamt of doing other things like studying photography, which had always been at the back of his mind, but his busy work and other commitments had ruled his life.

When I walked through the home, he told me how he had taken many photos of all the places in the world he had been to and said he yearned to study the subject a little more, but never had the time because of all his other commitments and priorities to his family. Now that he had the time, I suggested he follow his dreams and turn the empty, lonely looking bedroom, which used to be his son's room until he moved overseas (this was in the *inner knowledge/intuition* section) into a small man cave, decorate it with his collections of lovely paintings, set up a work desk with a computer, and get to following his dreams.

He had wanted to do photography for years so I suggested this would be the perfect place to set it up and perhaps if he wanted he could also turn it into an enterprising business.

Thrilled to bits at my suggestion he thought about it for a few seconds and laughed out loud, thanking me for the inspiration, as it was something that he was thinking about doing for quite a while. This was a perfect opportunity at a new way of life to keep him happy in his golden days.

CASE STUDY: **Susan**

Susan was a naturopath with a busy practice in the city. She ran her business really well, was always doing new courses to keep her knowledge up-to-date, but she never made time for herself at the end of the day. She was always tired and grumpy.

Susan was thinking of cutting back her hours, giving her staff more responsibility, and working part-time so she could write a few books as she had learnt so much wisdom over the years, but every time she thought of doing other things she would always go blank and could not feel inspired or think.

When she rang me, she wasn't sure why this was the case, but intuitively felt that I could help her unblock her energy and mind, and get to the next level of her life and where she wanted to go.

As soon as I arrived and walked around the large office, I could see why Susan was so successful with her business as she was very organised, clean and efficient. The only thing that bothered me was that her rooms were so stuffy; there was poor ventilation and on a psychic level, there was a terrible, suffocating presence of a heavy, toxic cloud of thick energy that lingered in every room.

To me, this was a massive build-up of toxic energy that she had not remembered to clear after each client at the end of a session. The other thing that bothered me was the pungent smell of strong herbs, oils and treatments that obviously never bothered her, but lingered unpleasantly in the air.

When you work with the general public and all their problems, especially when they are sick, have blocked energy, and diseases, it is always important to unclutter and clear the energy by giving the place a good smudging with some sage and gum leaves. This will clear the air and space of all negativity in every nook and cranny. Another suggestion to renew energies and clear the chi in the rooms, is to walk slowly around each section of the office in the morning and ring a small brass bell, play a crystal bowl, or gong a Tibetan brass bowl to get the energy going. This will clear any negative clutter in the air and bring peace and harmony to your workroom. I have done this many times with great success, not only in my own office but also in healing centres over the years. A good dose of fresh air is very important and I cannot stress how this will change and clear an atmosphere within seconds. Stale and dirty air, even with an atomiser, creates bad feng shui energy, and is not good for the health, spirit, or mind.

Many times, with my over-sensitive and psychic nose, waiting to see someone in their waiting rooms can be difficult, especially if the air is bad and stuffy, and I can smell the old and worn carpet on the ground.

I also suggested that after seeing each patient, she set up *portholes,* or columns of light, in the corner of her workroom to remove the wasted energy that is no longer needed, wash her hands, and then dry them on a clean towel afterwards. This would be her way of replenishing herself and not taking on the client's energy.

Once I had given the information to Susan, she was very grateful and thanked me for reminding her of all the things she knew, but had forgotten to implement.

## FAMILY/HEALTH SECTION

The *east* section of the home is all about the support you need in your life with family and loving, supportive friendships. This area of your home is unique. It is what I call the 'spiritual foundation of the home', and when filled with positive energy and balance, it should bring you great harmony and confidence with your abilities. People should see you in the world without criticism or judgement.

The *east* is also the *health* section of your home and at all times needs to be uncluttered and kept fresh. It is located next to the *inner knowledge* and *intuition* section of the home; the middle section on the left hand side of your home.

## CASE STUDY: Ronny

Ronny was a mother at my daughter's school that I became friends with over the years. She was a lovely woman from Wales and had three children. One day, she overheard me talking to another friend about the importance of feng shui and space clearing, and asked if I could come over one day after school and give her a few tips. Her family was having money worries and going through a difficult time.

After a cup of tea and a good laugh, I began to walk around her lovely home and got a shock when I came to the *health* section, as it was a room that was locked and not used. Asking her to open the door, I nearly fell backwards as it was dark and smelled of rotting papers. The whole room was filled with boxes full of papers and junk.

When I asked her if anyone was suffering from illness in the family, she looked at me shocked. She said her husband had been ill for months and had just been recently diagnosed with terminal cancer. Not knowing what to say, we both looked at each other and Ronny started to cry.

Giving her a hug, I gently suggested that perhaps it might be a good idea to activate the section of the house, as her husband would need all the help he could get. She lit a white candle she had in a cupboard in the kitchen, and then I said a little prayer asking spirit for help.

We cleared the room together the next day, and then I bought around some lovely lavender and an oil burner to get rid of the sickly smell. I also gave her a lucky gold Buddha and a green money plant for the room as well.

A couple of months later, Ronny rang me and thanked me for my kindness and said that the family were moving back home to Wales for support. Unfortunately, I heard through the grapevine that her husband passed a few years later.

### CASE STUDY: **Bonne**

Bonne had a fish and chip business that she loved. She ran it with her husband. They had inherited it from her family and she had worked there for most of her life. Her husband Josh was a fisherman and liked to do his own thing, so she was alone in the shop most of the time. She loved her work and what she did, and because of her happy disposition, people always came back. The shop was successful and busy all the time, but at the end of the day, she never seemed to make a great deal of money.

She wanted to make a few improvements, so she rang me up and asked if I could come out and give her some pointers. On first impression, I could not find anything wrong. Everything was clean, neat, and tidy and I could not fault it in any way. I could sense the proud generations of her family that had worked together as a unit to keep the place busy.

On closer inspection though, I noticed that she had several leaks in her *health* section from the taps in the bathroom. I could hear the steady sound of dripping water all the time, and when I asked her about her pipes she complained it was an old building and they often had blocked drains, especially when it rained. She had asked her husband several times to fix it but he was always so busy. When I told her this was not good and she needed to fix these things, she said she had been thinking of making improvements as the building was old and needed quite a few repairs. She was happy to do this but kept putting it off because of the family commitments and busy work schedule.

To me, the place had a really lovely energy but just needed a bit of old-fashioned tender loving care, as everything just seemed a bit drab, worn-out and old. I suggested a good paint job, and an inspirational picture on wall to greet people when they came in.

## WEALTH SECTION

The *wealth* section of the home is always in the *south-east* section of the home. The energy of wealth is the *'richness of the soul'* in your life and is all about abundance, the universal law of attraction, and the ability to receive harmony and balance in every aspect of your life. This is the section of the home that reminds us to be open to receiving abundance and wealth on every level.

CASE STUDY: **Karen and John**

Karen and John were having problems saving money. They both worked very hard but were big spenders and unable to save. When I walked into the far left section of their home, all I could see was washing all over the place, with an old ironing board set up in the middle of the room and untidiness and clutter everywhere. The room was also closed and felt very stuffy, with hardly any light coming in.

When I commented about what I was seeing and feeling, Karen starting complaining and told me that she never had time to do anything, did not think she was worthy of having a good life, and kept putting herself down.

This worried me so I suggested she try the art of positive thinking, and begin to acknowledge and write good things about her everyday life. I then explained how to do mirror work. By looking at her reflection and telling herself she was a beautiful person and deserved the best always, this would gradually help to change her thought forms.

To activate her *wealth* section, I also suggested that she open the blinds to let the light in, to air the room out every day, and then I suggested some good cures. These were placing something with a purple power colour, like a cloth, to cover up her washing basket, buying a large Amethyst crystal to place on the empty shelf, and placing a pot of bamboo in the corner of the room. As it grew, so too did her wealth.

I also suggested the *career* section needed a once over, and advised on a few cures there like a small water fountain that would get the energy going, and an inspirational picture to make this section feel important.

CASE STUDY: **Kathy**

Kathy was a kind, gentle, and compassionate vet who ran a busy business for years. She was very well-respected in the industry with a good reputation, and she thoroughly enjoyed her work like most successful people in the world.

Unfortunately, things took a turn for the worse and everything changed when a very angry, obnoxious man decided to set up a small handyman business next door. No sooner had he arrived, he began to think that he was now in charge and began to take delight in complaining all the time, causing nothing but trouble.

This behaviour seemed to go on relentlessly, day after day, as he found something else he that he thought was wrong, like the dogs that barked, or awful, strange smells coming from her place, or anything petty, damaging and ridiculous that could cause stress.

Eventually, this toxic energy had a terrible effect, not only on Kathy, but also her staff. They were all badly affected and wanted to leave. Over time the once prosperous business started to go down, and Kathy starting losing not only her focus, but her beloved, once loyal staff who, understandably, were sick of the fighting all the time.

Not knowing what to do and at her wits end, she gave me a ring and asked if there was any way I could help her deal with the problem, as she had no intention of moving and was going broke.

Once I arrived, I could feel the very heavy, stressful energy in the air. I could understand, sympathetically, exactly what the poor woman was going through.

The first thing I did was tune into the energy in the space, and I could see that the man next door, who was a bully, had caused trouble before with other people and was hell-bent on getting her out.

After walking through the whole place, I gave Kathy my report. The first thing I suggested was to place a few Bagua mirrors on outside walls, facing his premises. Once we had done this, a lot of the aggressive, negative energy would stop as it would be blocked by the mirrors.

Then I suggested boundaries was a good thing, so I thought perhaps my *Higher Self* meditation (found in chapter 6) would be excellent for this situation, as it always works and has helped many people I have seen over the years. When I told her this, she thought it was a good idea as she hated confrontations and had no desire to speak to him. Talking to him spiritually, in a meditation, sounded a lot better than to try and talk reason to the man.

The next things we did were activate the *wealth* sector and the *fame* sector. I suggested a water feature for the small courtyard and a tiny wind chime. The next thing to do, if none of this worked fast enough, was to be practical and write a letter to the council to tell them of his behaviour.

A few months later, Kathy rang me out of the blue. She was happy and said things had quietened down. She was relieved as she did not have to worry anymore, nor did she have to ring or write to the council, as the angry man had, for some strange reason, suddenly given up on making her life hell and making complaints all the time.

## FAME AND REPUTATION SECTION

The *fame* and *reputation* section of the home is next to the *wealth* section and is located in *south* corner of your home. This section is all about how you are recognised, appreciated, and rewarded in your world by family, friends and the broader community. It is all about how others see you in your world; with reward, recognition, and appreciation.

### CASE STUDY: Julie

Julie was a single, hard-working career woman who worked as a journalist for a TV station. She was always travelling around the place, covering news stories for her show. She had been doing the same thing for years and always felt, begrudgingly, that she was never fully recognised or rewarded for her hard work, especially when other colleagues who were doing the same thing were always getting the lucky breaks.

When she rang me up for help, I headed to the *fame* section of her home and was not impressed. All I could see was a drab, lonely room with an old lounge in the middle and old packets of half-eaten potato chips strewn across it. There was a small table in the middle of the room full of old shabby magazines, rubbish, and empty coke cans.

I suggested it might be a good idea to clean up her mess, place a vase of sweet smelling red flowers on the table, and introduce some red pillows on the lounge. On her sideboard against the wall, which was empty, I suggested a few cures like a small water fountain for movement in the *north* section of the room, and a large quartz crystal to program to bring success and abundance. Taking it a step further, I told her to get a picture of herself that she loved and place in on the sideboard with a gold star next to it for 'star power', so she could be recognised in the world.

If anything, the room needed creative energy and with the simple cures I gave her, there would be deserving rewards for her hard work and more opportunities would come in.

CASE STUDY: **Bianca**

Bianca was a delightful young girl who sang in a band and wanted to be famous and travel all over the world with her gifts. She wanted to make people happy as music was her first and greatest love. Ever since she was little, she had always dreamed of seeing herself on a huge stage and being a successful entertainer, but she never seemed to have any luck or recognition as she always ended up with the wrong people that never had the same dreams and ambitions as herself.

The guys she was playing with in her band at the time I met her, were, according to her, very good musicians, even though she wrote most of the songs and music alone; but they were definitely not on the same wavelength as they lacked the same drive and ambition that she had. They seemed pleasant enough, but according to Bianca they were unmotivated, lazy, drank too much, and were more interested in chasing women.

When I arrived at her small flat, I could see just by taking a quick look around that she was very organised as everything was neat and tidy. The only thing that I felt she needed to concentrate on was herself and nobody else, like she had always done in the past, because sometimes it is the *people* we work with that are the clutter that stops us from moving forward with all our dreams.

Once I explained this to her, she laughed and said she understood, as she intuitively had been thinking the same thing. I suggested we activate the *career* section, the *helpful people* section for networking and the *fame* section as they could all work for her quite well. After discussing simple cures for her home, I told her to get a vision board and write all her dreams down with a time frame, but not too far in the future.

Within three months of these suggestions, she rang me in excitement, hysterically laughing, and said that she had got a job as a singer in an international band on a luxury cruiser which travelled all over the world. Thrilled to bits and thanking me repeatedly, she was eternally grateful to know that she was finally on her way to fame and great success.

## RELATIONSHIP SECTION

The *relationship, romance* and *marriage* section is located in the *south-west* corner of your home. It is important to apply the grid to your bedroom as well as your home, as this is all about harmony and love. I always suggest a pair of anything, like mandarin ducks or anything that you like as a pair in this section, as it is always a good, safe cure.

For the bedroom, always make the theme romantic. If you're looking for love, or no matter how long you have been married, make it romantic and have soft colours as your main theme; a bit of red or leopard print for spicy romance, and a rose quartz crystal to bring in more harmony and love.

If your bathroom is located in this section, it could mean that you have difficult relationships. To remedy the situation, introduce Wood and Metal colours and objects to reduce the negative impact.

CASE STUDY: **John**

John was having problems in his love life. No matter how hard he tried to have a happy relationship, it always ended in a *Fatal Attraction* type of disaster. Either they were not interested in him or he met the wrong type, so it was not surprising that when he rang me up, he sounded depressed and ready to give up on his dream of having a happy relationship or marriage.

When I walked into his home, it almost made me laugh when I saw that the *relationship* section of his home was mainly in the small dark toilet and extended laundry at the far right section of his home. When I pointed this out, he nearly had a heart attack and desperately begged me to help him. It all sounded like a very sad story and a 'what's the point' situation, so I quickly reassured him, enthusiastically and happily, that it was certainly not a problem with simple feng shui cures and magical, practical solutions.

For a start, I told him that it would be a good idea to keep the toilet door closed to avoid unpleasant smells, and to always keep the toilet clean with the lid down. I asked him to give the area a good scrub and get rid of any clutter, especially in the cupboard; things like old pegs, lost underpants, odd socks, and empty packets of washing detergent.

Then, for a cure, I suggested he place a pair of something that he loved in the *south-west* corner of the living room. While it's not a good idea to activate elements in a bathroom, you can use the living room to activate the elements of a particular section. Most people I have worked with prefer the old and successful idea of mandarin ducks but John, being a bush man, loved birds so I suggested he get two little statues of love parrots, and to give them names, making sure that one was a boy and one a girl. Also, in the right section of the room near the window, I told him to hang a tiny metal wind chime so every time the wind blew, you would hear a gentle, lovely chime. Creating music and ambience in the space would exhaust the Earth element. There was also enough room to place a Wood cure, a bamboo plant, as there was plenty of light and space in the laundry section.

When I asked permission to see his bedroom, it did not take me long to work out that he was extremely lonely. As soon as I walked into his room, I was swallowed up by a very heavy, depressing, and sad energy. Walking further into the room, if I had not known any better, I would have thought he was a monk, or I was standing in a prison cell. My eyes just about popped out of my head when I saw nothing but bare cold walls and a single bed squeezed into a corner of the room. On the other side of the room, there was also a small, plain, unimpressive cupboard, a picture of a grey and bleak landscape which did nothing for the imagination, and a small table which stood all alone with a small cartoon lamp. His mother must have given it to him when he was ten.

Not commenting too much on what I saw, I gently suggested to get rid of the old and bring in the new energy waiting for him around the corner, and perhaps spice it up a bit with some cures that he would like from my selection.

The first thing I suggested was that he should think about getting a bigger bed, as when he did meet someone, on a practical level, there would be nowhere for them to sleep. Then I told him he had permission to use his incredible imagination and taste to make his room more romantic, like in the movies, so his private quarters could be something special for his new lover or soul mate who were ready and waiting to come in.

I also wanted him to feel blessed and full of gratitude every day, so that every morning, when he opened his eyes to a new day, he would feel like the 'king of the world' — pampered, nurtured, and loved. My other cures were some large, soft pillows for decoration to match the new creamy doona cover that went with his new king-sized bed, and some beautiful romantic and inspiring pictures on the wall. As for the cartoon lamp he was given when he was it kid, it had to go, and in its place on the small table was a lovely white lamp with soft blues, pinks, and reds on it, a pair of purple mandarin ducks, and a large rose quartz crystal. A few months later, John rang me up, very excited, and thanked me enthusiastically for my advice, which he doubted at first, but things were now looking onwards and upwards in the romance department and in his social life. He told me that he had, just by chance, met a fantastic, beautiful, and funny woman he could not get enough of at a work conference. They were now in constant contact and had dated more than a dozen times. They were also planning their first overseas trip together at the end of the year.

I was happy to hear the good news, especially when he told me that his mother, who he was close to, was extremely grateful for my help as well. She had given up on him, and now wanted to make me one of her cakes! After the phone call, I had a large smile on my face, happy to know my good and trusted cures had done their job so well.

### CASE STUDY: Harry

Harry was a client who owned a timber yard and was having problems in every aspect of his life. He had split up from his wife, didn't see his grown-up children, and was now experiencing not only problems with money and business, but also trouble with his neighbours and the local council.

When I spoke to him on the phone, I could sense he was a non-believer in what I did, but was weary and open for change. One of his friends, a woman neighbour, had heard about me and the work I did from friends of hers, so she insisted he give me a go as he was at his wits end, and tired of struggling all the time.

When I arrived at the five acres of pristine rural property, I listened quietly while Harry told me all his troubles. He told me, in his gruff way, that his home was in complete chaos after he decided to block the creek running at the back of his property while major renovations were in progress. This natural stream had been there for as long as anyone could remember and had never been disturbed before. Why he foolishly decided to do this was beyond me. Clearly, his actions did not go unnoticed by all the elemental and nature spirits that had been living there forever. It was no wonder his life had changed dramatically. It was now a constant struggle with things going inexplicably wrong.

Within days of obstructing the little creek, Harry's once peaceful home became a war zone with angry neighbours, unreliable workmen, and obstructions from the council. He was also having electrical breakdowns, telephone, and power circuit disruptions, not to mention blocked pipes and sewerage issues. The disputes, continuing negative energy, and general bad luck had become overwhelming, he said, and it was beginning to cost him a fortune. It did not take him long to realise that he was way out of his depth. Everything around him began to seem like a nightmare and his health soon began to suffer from the stress. Harry had called me in as a last resort.

I tuned into the situation and immediately saw the build-up of energy that was out of balance in the home and surrounding yard. On entering the home, I also encountered an earthbound spirit, an elderly man who had been living in the house since it was built and was upset with the disruption. He said he was unhappy with all the noise, and could not understand what was going on in what he still thought was his home.

Once I explained that he needed to go into the light and sent him on his way, I had the nature spirits to contend with. This was not so simple as the client had to unblock the stream, which took a few days, and I had to say many prayers of love and appreciation to the nature spirits, who appeared as tiny little orbs surrounding the creek, to reassure them that the stream would never be harmed again. My spirit guide instructed me to ask for forgiveness from the elders of the land who were the traditional Aboriginal owners, and to ask for a blessing for my client and his home. As I did, the atmosphere seemed much less frenetic, although Harry reported it took another week or so before everything settled back down to a peaceful state again, and he was happy to use a few of the cures that I suggested as well.

## CREATIVE/ CHILDREN/PROJECTS SECTION

This space, important like every other section in our home, is located in the *west* corner of the home, next to the *relationships* and *helpful people* section. It's also an important space to earmark in a bedroom. This energy is about activating balance and bliss your life, play and awakening our creative spirit. This is also a great place to show photos of the family and kids artwork. Often in feng shui, growing a white flowering plant in this section can promote growth in spiritual pursuits and creative endeavors.

### CASE STUDY: **Vanessa**

Vanessa was a client of mine who was desperate to have a baby. She had tried many times through IVF and had spent a large amount of money in the past. Her husband and family were desperate for her to have children, and every day she felt sad and disappointed as she never seemed to be able to conceive, no matter what she did.

Vanessa had endured many tests throughout her younger years but unfortunately, the doctors, in the end, could not understand why she never fell pregnant. After a while, it was suggested she might want to go and see a psychologist before she decided to go any further, as there were concerns that she was carrying an emotional problem. After reading some literature on past life regression, Vanessa contacted me to see if I could give her insight to her problem and clear the issue through regression through the ages and spiritual healing.

When we did the past life regression, she saw herself as a young Indian woman, around the same age she was today, with her three children in a simple canoe made from the oak trees along the river. The family seemed to be travelling very fast in the dangerous and wild current, and before too long, the small canoe lost control as it struck a rock and capsized, drowning everyone aboard. The last memory that Vanessa witnessed before her own mortal death, was the horror at having to watch helpless as her three beloved children drowned. After her own untimely death, her loving guide arrived and took her to the spirit world, where she was once again able to meet her children who were all waiting for her.

This healing had a powerful effect on Vanessa. When I went to her house a few months later, she seemed a different person and told me in no uncertain terms that she was ready to have children, as the unknown fear had left her.

One of the cures I suggested was to put green sheets on her bed as this was good for fertility. Colour is always an inspirational cure for many purposes, depending on the section of the home. When I am doing healing on clients, I always suggest using white sheets as this brings in healing from our own team of spirit doctors that we can work with in meditation. When I walked into the *creative/children/projects* section of the home, I told Vanessa to brighten the room and make it more fun, as this was used as a formal sitting room and was far too stuffy. She was always interested in drawing and painting, so I suggested that she use the space as an artistic and sacred space for her own creativity and writing. I told her to play with the energy, decorate it as she wished, and to use some of the cures from her own intuition, and what she was drawn to.

The last time I heard from Vanessa and her husband, she rang me up and told me she was having twins. She was excited! She knew in her heart that everything would go well, as she was no longer fearful. She was ready.

### CASE STUDY: Juliet

Juliet was a hardworking osteopath that specialised in all types of injuries of the spine and back. She was very successful, but she was a workaholic who never had any time to have a social life. She had decided long ago that she wanted to be by herself, but was ready now to have a bit of fun and do things in a different way.

Her mother, who she was very close to, had just died and so she made an important lifestyle decision to make change. When I arrived at her office, which she ran from the side of her home, I could not get over how impersonal the whole place was. It was like she lived and breathed only for her work. The whole *creative/children* section really needed some work as it was stacked with bookcases, and looked very much like a formal library. There were so many aspects to talk about in her lonely and cold home, so we spent a few hours deciding what we should do when I applied the Bagua, as it was time for her to take charge and move on with her new life.

The first thing was to get rid of was all the clutter she had stored everywhere, and to get rid of her deceased mother's things like her old wheelchair, walking sticks, and commode, which sat in the middle of the lounge room. The plan we made would take a while, but she was happy with the suggestions and placement of many things.

After a period of six months, she rang me up and gave me some feedback. After I left, she removed all of her mother's old stuff and felt a whole lot better. She also had decided to buy a new lounge, one that she had been looking at for quite a while. Her home, she told me, was still a project in progress, but she could not believe how much fun she was having when placing certain cures in areas around her house.

## HELPFUL PEOPLE/TRAVEL SECTION

The *helpful people* and *travel* section is located in the *north-west* section of the home. This section helps to network with good people who can bring great connections and support into your life, form strong boundaries, and travel to fantastic destinations in the world. If you need help from the universe, this is the place to enhance with white, silver, grey, and gold colours and objects and crystals.

### CASE STUDY: **Elizabeth**

Elizabeth was an up and coming actress that was always having problems with her career. She had been in show business for years but was always failing at her auditions and never getting the big breaks. She was also unhappy with her agent who never seemed to put her up for anything.

She was happily married but was frustrated with her career at the time I saw her, so as soon as I got to her home, it was interesting to see that most of the *helpful people* section, so good for networking, seemed to be cut off or missing, due to the shape of the home. When this happens it is an easy thing to rectify with simple cures, so I suggested going outside the home and into the small courtyard, where we placed a wind chime, a golden Buddha, and a green succulent in a terracotta pot. When she asked me why I had chosen the succulent, I replied that as she watered the plant and it steadily grew, she would see more and more people come into her life and offer her help.

Not long afterwards, she was given the name of a really good agent and finally landed a job in a travelling show.

# CHAPTER 5

## *Feng Shui at Work*

Let's face it, ever since we were little, just about everyone has dreamt of achieving success in their lives or being recognised for what they do in their work and career. This includes not only you, but all the top-notch executives and famous people in the world who are always striving to make it to the next level.

Being successful means having great recognition for the brilliant work you do, and if you love your job, no matter how humble you are, you will always be rewarded and create good fortune as you are working with positive universal chi energy. Nobody wants to work hard, struggle to achieve success, and not be able to make a profit. Life in the fast lane can be exhausting, but with good planning and strategies, we can create the life we want to live with great enthusiasm, belief in ourselves, and getting into the groove of positive thinking in our working lives.

Everyone loves a winner and nobody wants to work with disgruntled co-workers that do nothing but complain, gossip and steal your energy. These type of energy drainers usually end up being resentful of everything you do, and usually end up doing nothing with their lives as it is all too hard. At the end of the day, all they care about is themselves anyway. The only way they would be happy in their lives is if it was handed to them on a silver platter.

Success does not grow on trees, it has to be earned and with things in mind like careful planning, a positive attitude, and becoming a team player. Knowing a few helpful feng shui principles can get you on your way, especially if you learn how to play with energy, create peace and balance in your life, then you can have the life that you desire. With a positive attitude, good boundaries and a passion for what you do, you can create a better working life. Believe in your dreams. I really believe that by taking charge of your life, you can excel in any given area or aspect that you need or want. Why not become the driver of your own life instead of just being a passenger in the back seat, bumbling along, and not really caring or taking any responsibility?

From a feng shui perspective, it is always important to have a clutter-free office. Clutter is toxic, is a waste of space, and reflects worry as it acts as an obstacle. It stops energy from flowing freely. This can cause tiredness, fatigue, a lack of motivation, and an unpleasant work environment. A cluttered space reflects a cluttered mind. When you clear your space, you will be able to think more clearly, positive energy will flow, and your space will be ready for new and improved work opportunities.

## GOING FOR THE DREAM JOB

Looking for a new job and going for interviews can be a very stressful time, no matter where you are in your career. It is not only a means to reach an income, but also a form of social interaction and inclusion, and a use of all your talents, knowledge, wisdom, abilities, and gifts.

If you happen to be over fifty, it is even worse because everyone likes to tell you negative information and give you bad chi. *Aren't you are too old? Give it up! Why don't you think about retiring?*

Wake up everyone!

The world, as we know, is forever changing all the time. The old fifty is the new forty, so get used to it and go with the flow. Always keep a positive attitude and you will get the job you deserve, so stay optimistic and never second-guess yourself. See it in your mind's eye and nurture yourself by exercising, eating fresh and unprocessed food, and staying in a clean and healthy state of chi energy. You can create your own destiny and design the life you want to live, so give yourself a break and don't listen to what other people say. Good feng shui in your working life is not just about a good resume and hanging something by your door, it is about attitude, spirituality, and your own consciousness with positive thinking.

When going for a job, it is always important to give a good impression and stretch your limits. No matter how you feel on the day, fill your mind with powerful affirmations and know, trust, and feel that you are the best person for the job, no matter how stressful and doubtful you are. Set up your wishes and desires and believe in them, as they will be fulfilled. I don't know how many people I know that are very hardworking, talented, and good at their job, but when it comes to interviews they always fail, and are depressed and unhappy with their performance on the day.

Always know that you deserve what you need in your life, and you are the best person. Remember, the three C's: *commitment, confidence,* and *courage*. You can do things you never believed were possible. You can achieve great things — don't dream about your life — do it. Take a leap of faith and believe in yourself.

Remember the golden mantra, "*I am the best person for this job.*" A job is not only a means to an income; it is about your future, and is a form of social inclusion for all your gifts, talents, and remarkable abilities.

Impressions are important, so always dress in a professional manner and smile as it shows you are confident, intelligent, and pleasant. Whatever you do, don't turn up dressed as a Goth, rock star, or some type of new age artist with piercings everywhere. I don't care what you do underneath your clothing, each to their own, but this is a job. No matter how cool or incredible *you think you are,* people are always looking at what you are wearing, especially in the workforce, so make sure you are neat, tidy, and impeccably dressed from head to toe.

I once knew an actress that always wore red lipstick, dressed in red underpants, and wore red shoes all the time to make an impression when she went for auditions. It must have worked for her, because she ended up being very successful in her career. Every time I tried to contact her to catch up for a coffee, she was always working and travelling all over the place.

Make sure you are clean, scrubbed, not sweaty, and feeling like a million dollars. Bad, terrible smells, like poor body odour, bad breath, and excessive aftershave or heavy perfumes are an absolute, capital N-O in the workforce as they can cause bad chi energy, and they do not give a good impression. I once knew a woman that had rotten teeth and bad breath. When she complained all the time about never getting a proper job, I suggested that she might try to spend a bit of time and money on her appearance. Unfortunately, we do live in a visual world and first impressions are, no matter what anyone says, important. When I told her this, she said she was thinking along the same lines. She was fed up with her life and had actually booked into a good dentist to get some false teeth.

Crystals are good to have on the body as not only are they beautiful, but they can be positive amplifiers of incredible energy. They can be used to keep you calm, protect you, and help you be in charge if you know how to use them. Their properties are very soothing and healing. Always be careful using them though, because they are amplifiers of energy. If you are fearful, they can project this. Whenever I go for a job, I always wear my diamond stud earrings and place a small rose quartz close to my heart. This can be done by tucking it into your bra, if you're a woman, or wearing it in a pocket, if you are a man.

Always turn up early, say twenty minutes before, to steady those nerves. There is nothing worse than arriving late as you can lose all your preparation. This will also create good chi, as your employer will think you are eager and very professional.

Before going for a job, do your research and understand all there is to know about the position you want, the people you may be working for, and exactly what your role may be. Never go unprepared, always do your homework, and if anything, always be ready for the unexpected.

Before going for a new job that will ultimately change your lifestyle and get you on the road to success, it is always good to get rid of any clutter in your home and office as they correspond to each other. This includes your over-stuffed cupboards of clothes and accessories that have long outlived their use-by date, and any rubbish that may be stored under your bed. When you have done this, check your desk for papers, untidy files, food leftovers, and any type of toxic rubbish which may be stopping the natural flow of chi energy in your life. Look also at the *career*, *helpful people* and *wealth* sections of your home so that you can energise and give yourself a new start.

## IN THE OFFICE

An uninspiring office space leads to a lack of creativity and procrastination, which is not very helpful if you have a long to-do list. A messy, cluttered office space contains scattered energy that affects your ability to think clearly and focus on your goals. Good feng shui can reward you with the ability to think more clearly and focus on what is important, like achieving your career goals. When you are working in a supportive environment you will feel settled, focused and more in control. Your external surroundings mirror what's going on internally, and by harmonising and changing your surroundings, you can make positive changes to your life and improve your well-being.

## POWER POSITION

Always sit in a position of power and authority, so place your chair in a position where you can see the door and people that are entering your office space. This will always provide a sense of security.

## BE ORGANISED

Always have an organised office by making sure that all of your files are in order, easily accessible and not lying all over the place, like on the floor. Also, sit with your back to a solid wall as this will provide backing and support for all your ideas. If this is not possible, try placing a partitioned screen behind your chair.

## BAGUA

Place the Bagua map at the entrance of your office, start from the front door and imagine your office divided in sections. You can also do this with the building, your office, and your desk. The object in business feng shui is to create a balanced environment that motivates staff and clients, and to activate the wealth sector at the far right corner of the room to improve prosperity.

## PROTECTION

If you are feeling sensitive in the workforce, always place a protective barrier or shield around you. You can also do this to your loved ones as well as your home and possessions. If you are having a really hard time, as extra protection, try using gold light as well. Just imagine, in your mind's eye, the energy as the sun and wrap it around your body and aura, dissolving any darkness or shadows.

## BOUNDARIES

Exercise strong boundaries with everyone in your life. Sometimes, that may include family and loved ones. Our biggest teachers to take us on the rollercoaster of life are sometimes our own siblings or close friends, not just people we hardly know. Always listen to your intuition. It is never wrong, and is in fact your own higher self, or soul energy, talking to you. We also have our own guides and angel helpers to give us a hand as well — so do not think for one minute that you are ever alone. I don't know how many times I have heard people say to me that they had a feeling or thought something was wrong, or they felt the situation wasn't right in their gut. These moments of truth are real and are honest and totally amazing. Trust and listen to your own feelings, always, as they are never wrong. Sometimes the subconscious mind will show us the answers to problems in our dreams when we are asleep or in meditation.

## HOW TO ENERGISE YOUR DESK

Start with placing your Bagua map over your desk and imagine it divided into the allocated sections. By doing this we can see what sections of the desk we need to energise. At all times, always make sure your desktop is clean and tidy, like your office. Never have clutter on your desk because a lack of organisation reflects a cluttered and unorganised mind. Removing obstacles on the desk enables you to think more clearly.

On your computer, place a large crystal on top for good chi energy, and especially for recognition for the good work you do. If you have a website, make sure it's currently serviced, user friendly, up-to-date, modern and engaging.

A website is important as it is a strong element of feng shui for modern times. Your screensaver should reflect something either motivational or inspirational for you.

Never have anything negative, violent, or depressing like pictures on your desk that may have influence. I always have inspirational quotes and decoration on my desk, and a lucky elephant facing the door which I intuitively feel helps create positive energy to come my way. I also have a picture of Jesus, an angel, and a statue of the goddess Isis representing spiritual assistance. As my writing desk is so big, wide, and spacious, I also have a selected arrangement of some beautiful crystals as I am open to their healing energies.

A vision board is a good thing to have as it is motivational and keeps you on track with all your goals. To the side of my desk, I have a vision board that I am able to change when I reach my desired goals. Another good tip is to have a mirror. As you look in the mirror before you start your day, look into your eyes and give yourself an affirmation that you may use to help you with your projects. My desk is always neat, tidy, and functional because every time I sit down to write I am always full of energy, which is a positive and good thing.

## ATMOSPHERE

Always have fresh air and natural light in your office. Many offices have fixed windows so sometimes it is not possible, but if you work from home, try to ventilate it as much as possible. Opening windows and blinds will always help to renew the energy in your office, and fresh air is vital as it improves health and concentration.

If possible, use a spray for relaxation with essential oils such as lavender, rose, geranium, and sandalwood. Put a few drops of the selected oils you wish to work with in a small bottle with water, so you can spray it when wanted. You can also use a small burner and place water and a few small drops for an ambient feel, creating harmony in your office space.

## PLANTS

Fresh flowers or plants are wonderful for fresh chi energy and are uplifting. These could be placed on the top section of your desk if possible. If you don't have fresh flowers, try bamboo or a green succulent plant as this will improve your air quality and bring harmony and money. Plants are great for boosting health and energy levels in a study or an office. Plants such as the peace lily have broad leaves to effectively produce oxygen and remove chemicals from your indoor air. Never use fake plants or plastic flowers as they are dead energy and will just become collectors of dirt and dust.

## IMAGES

Place an inspirational picture on the wall behind you to bring in good chi energy. This could be a calming picture, or a magnificent picture of a strong mountain that can be inspirational for you to reach great heights.

Surround yourself with beautiful things, such small pictures, inspirational quotes or statues of things that you love and adore.

## COLOUR

Be aware of colours in your study or place of work. Each colour has its own healing powers. Beige, rose, lavender, and green are good colours to alleviate negative vibes. Gold décor encourages trust and loyalty. Too much white creates sterility and a perfectionist, unrelenting mind. The colour yellow is productive as it is helpful to promote thinking and concentration. Go easy on blues as they will calm you too much and make you sleepy. Also, too much red will be over-stimulating and may give you headaches, but it can be used on chairs or upholstery, as this definitely puts workers in the hot seat due to the highly stimulating colour. This can drive people to higher performances. A base of cream is good to use as you can then introduce other colours such as rose, dark blues, and oranges, especially in larger offices. Purple is a regal colour and is great to use in the executive office, if that is where you want to go. A rich royal purple, for example, gives an impression of big ideas and creativity.

## LIGHTING

Always have adequate lighting, as the office space is very important. Always place your desk where there is abundant natural light, and use warm lighting at night as it more closely resembles daylight. Downlights and incandescent globes are examples of warm lighting whereas florescent lights are examples of cold and harsh lighting. Never work in in a dark or dim area as this will cause strain on the eyes, and may impair the health of your eyesight later in life.

## ACCESSIBILITY

Avoid sitting near pointy objects and directly underneath low-sloped ceilings and low overhead beams. Moving your chair away from these structures can help you reduce tension and headaches.

Always place something attractive at your front entrance (the mouth) to draw the natural universal chi energy into your building or office. This could be a beautiful window display, a piece of artwork or a green plant with soft leaves. Never place anything spikey at the entrance of a home, workplace, or office.

Make sure people can find you if you have your own business or office, with the correct signage that people can easily see. Make sure you have clear street numbers too. I don't know how many times I have been on the road looking for my clients' premises, and have had problems finding where they live or their office. Whenever this happens I will always politely let them know this little fact, as often they do not understand why their business is always slow, and why they have problems with the general flow of good, successful, chi energy.

Always check for leaks, clogged drains, or dripping taps as this blocks the natural chi energy. Also, make sure there are no blown light bulbs, faulty electrical, or plumbing problems.

## CO-WORKERS

At all times be respectful, keep your own counsel, and be aware of your fellow workers. They are not your friends, but work colleagues. Use tact, guile, and diplomacy at all times, and remember the golden rule, *never sleep with the campers.* Just because you work with people every day does not mean that they are suddenly your best friends who want to hear about your problems and the dramas in your life. Always keep your own counsel and don't tell secrets that can be used against you.

There is nothing worse than bullying in the office, being on the receiving end of cruel gossip, plain rudeness, or bad manners. This creates bad chi energy for everyone who wants to be a team player. Be sensitive and courteous to others at all times, because remember, what goes around comes around.

A couple of years ago, a client came to me and told me how she helped an acquaintance who she knew from a past job, get a fantastic job where she was working. Thinking she was doing the right thing by helping this person and recommending him to everyone, she was sadly disappointed when the so-called friend used her as a stepping stone, and even went as far as pretending not to know the woman who helped him. The end result was that this created bad chi energy and before too long, the man found that the place was not good enough for him. The last she heard, he is still struggling.

As for the woman, she has learnt a valuable lesson in not giving all her own contacts away, and to concentrate on her own good luck and feng shui. It is always good to be gracious, have an open heart, and to help others, but sometimes, we need to stop and think before we jump into other people's dramas.

## OPEN PLAN OFFICES

Everyone thinks open plan offices are the ideal workplace these days, but sometimes they can cause stress for people, especially introverts, many of whom work better in their own private office.

Open plan offices are good to share information, as energy and ideas can flow faster, but many open plan offices are poorly designed, so it is important to have the right layout to help employees feel supported and valued. It is easier and more appropriate for people to work in private offices when they have a standalone role, or need a quiet environment for concentrating or conducting confidential meetings. People in this type of role would feel more stressed working in an open plan office as their environment is not supportive for what they need to achieve.

Hot-desking is a concept that can save business costs, however, this is not beneficial from a feng shui perspective as people are far less likely to feel connected to their workspace or feel like a valuable member of the team. Overall, a mix of open plan and private offices is healthy in a workspace as it creates a nice flow of balance.

If you work in an open plan office, try to sit with your back to a solid wall. If this is not possible then use a high-backed chair for extra support and protection. Not only will you save your posture, spine and health, you will feel comfortable, relaxed, supported, and be ready for your working day.

If you are sitting in an exposed position with your back to a busy walkway, have a reflective surface on your desk to reflect back some of the energy.

Create a space on your desk that is organised, easy to work with, and clean and tidy. Do not create negative chi by being thoughtless and spending endless hours on the web, your mobile, or social media. Consider your work colleagues and be more aware if others are working harder than you. Ask yourself if you are a team player. Believe it or not, others know what you are doing, even though you might not think so. Always have a professional standard and good ethics, and never abuse your power as this is negative chi and will come back at you in some way.

Use a lamp with an incandescent globe to create warm lighting as florescent lights are often found in open plan offices. Always keep workstations well organised, clean and clutter-free, and keep your work up-to-date and not piled up for later. Free your personal space of clutter.

Make every single day you go to work a new beginning, and be aware of everything around you. Let go of the things that went wrong the day before, as 'sweating the small stuff' can be draining. If you have had a poor energy day, give yourself a warm bath filled with Epsom salts or sea salt, to get rid of any negative energy or clutter you may have picked up from others in your energy field. A splash of lavender or sandalwood is good too, if you want to add essential oils. Always remember to shield yourself with a beautiful bubble of light from the universe, with a gold band wrapped around it for extra protection and as a shield from toxic energy. This is good feng shui and always works.

# CHAPTER 6

## *Healing*

*"Unsuccessful people live in fear. They hate, are envious, continually complain all the time, and are stuck in the 'poor me' energy. Successful people on the other hand, are blessed and operate at a more blissful, lighter vibration as they build each other up, encourage others less fortunate than themselves and attract wonderful opportunities in their life, thus living their lives to the fullest."*

*White Feather*

A toxic build-up of hatred, fear and negative energy can make you feel sick and miserable. It can be disempowering and extremely destructive as it disconnects us from the source and the innate divine power that we all have within us as souls. I call this debilitating, despicable energy the *dark force,* because it makes us feel lost and powerless. It not only sucks away our positive energy, but it also disconnects us from our goals, hopes and dreams, so much so, that it can affect our spiritual growth as an eternal soul.

Before we came to earth and reincarnated as souls, we all signed spiritual contracts in the spirit world to go through different experiences so we could learn the lessons we needed to grow as an eternal soul. Earth is like a big stage and we are the actors, creating our own realities. Unfortunately, some of the lessons we sign up for can be extremely unpleasant, especially when we are dealing with emotions and forces from outside that can also build up within. Jealousy, fear, greed, hatred, disapproval, revenge, denial, resistance, disgust, racial prejudice, and miscommunication are but a few. The effects of these disempowering emotions can cause disease in our energy centres and isolate us from a state of grace and love. They can send us into a state of fear, which is misinformation that, in turn, creates havoc in our lives.

Years ago when I was a trainee-nursing sister, there was a period of my training where I escorted cancer patients to Sydney for radiotherapy. In those days, the hospital where I worked did not have the proper facilities to treat these patients, so we had to take them on a special bus to the city for their therapy. Looking back, I will always remember those beautiful people and their very sad stories. All of them, although they were all from different walks of life, had suffered some type of emotional problem that they were never able to come to terms with. Each story was the same — they were full of sadness through some terrible incident that had happened to them. It used to make me wonder if this is why they got the cancer in the first place. Sometimes, these negative emotions and realities can be programmed into our minds from an early age. Because of this, we learn to give away our power. Our belief system creates our reality and how we live our life is our own choice. As an energy worker, I am always attracting people into my life as I am often called a beacon of light. Sometimes, these people end up being energy grabbers and before too long I find out that these are not the right people for me.

We have the power to choose the way we think and want to live our lives because of free will. We forget, or do not understand, that we are free as souls to make our own choices in life. In fact, we are free to make whatever choices we want; such as *I am happy, I am confident, I am a beautiful person*. The way our parents talk to us as children, with words such as, "Don't do that or the boogie man will get you", "What a shame you can't be like your brother", or "You will never amount to anything", and so on, is in reality, negative programming. Another way is when others talk negatively behind our backs or put us down in front of others to make their own egos feel more important.

Negative energy is all around us. It is even programmed into us by the media. How many times have you experienced this by simply reading the newspaper, or listening to the television or radio news telling us terrible things every day?

Ask yourself this question: How many of us are truly happy for our friends and colleagues when something good happens in their life and they become successful? Is it just human nature to be a bit jealous?

The other type of negative energy is via psychic attack, with someone sending us negative energy or thought forms. These attacks are very real and I have seen them often. In some cases, I have even heard of people using chanting to cause more harm to their intended target.

I find it hard to believe that people in different types of cultures, still, to this day, spend hours with angry, jealous thought forms, and even spend money buying curses so they can hurt the person they intend to destroy, or spend too many hours feeling unhappy for their friends or colleagues moving ahead. If they only knew they were wasting their time! The bad energy they are conjuring up only returns to them anyway. Just look at their personal lives and you will see that these people always suffer emotionally.

Whenever anything like this happens to you, just walk away and send them love. My work these days as an energy and light worker is not only in people's homes, but in helping people with their minds and belief systems. We need to understand that as eternal souls and spiritual people as a whole, we have choices in life. If anything, we need to learn how to speak to ourselves more lovingly so we can pass this love on to our friends, lovers, partners, and parents.

Once you are aware how energy works, you will never think or speak a negative word again as you become more aware of the law of attraction. What you give out comes back to you, so to speak, and most of us are unaware of how much power we have to influence our own lives. Here are a few statements we need to beware of.

## THE PATTERNS

I can't afford the petrol. I can't … I am not good enough.

I will try. No one is ever going to love me. Maybe tomorrow. Why should I? I am stupid. It's all their fault. So long as I get it cheaper and nobody finds out. I have always been like this.

Yeah sure, will do it later. I can't afford it, pay you back later. It is alright for you, you have a money tree in your backyard.

As a light worker, I honestly believe it is important to monitor your thoughts at all times. Most people, unless they are aware and work with energy, will have no idea how powerful their minds actually are, especially when it comes to energy. Negative beliefs and thought forms can be toxic and if left to build-up, they will attract more negative energy and bad experiences into their lives over time. Just like the old saying: *what you believe you become.*

A good habit to learn is to surround yourself with only positive, loving, and encouraging people, and always listen to *positive* thoughts only. Also, be aware of negative patterns in your life and mind. We create our own reality, so why not make it as positive and beautiful as possible? What's wrong with creating a beautiful heaven on earth? Negative, abusive people only take or steal our energy if we let them. They can only take us down a heavy, tiring path, leading us astray from our true spiritual purpose if we let them. Stay away from the self-pity people of the world as they can be draining too. These individuals are really miserable and toxic energy stealers.

Sometimes, a negative thought form will build-up in the aura, making us feel drained, ungrounded, and unhappy with ourselves. You can see this when you view the aura as it will look very dense. You can see the thought form appear above the crown chakra as a thick, dirty brown colour. We can also build up negative thought forms thinking that we are unworthy of long-term relationships. If this is not dealt with it will become part of a negative belief structure. To deal with this issue, visualise a beautiful pink bubble above your head and place all of your negativity into it. When it is full, simply surrender it to God and let it go.

Once you are aware of the negative self-talk, you will never again let another negative thought enter your head. Most of these thoughts stem from fear, or what is more commonly known as the *shadow side* of our personalities. They are simply patterns, and they can very easily enter your beautiful, creative mind and sabotage the good things in your life because *you* allow them to come in.

Most of these broken-down old programs can be thoughts we have carried since childhood. They have been buried deep within our subconscious minds for so long that they are a habit and now part of our reality. By simply changing the way you think and letting more joy, happiness, and love into your life, you can change your mindset and create miracles in your life. Do not ever be afraid of the real you and the powerful person inside of you. We are all divine souls and deserve so much more.

## EVERYBODY NEEDS LOVE

Most of the clients that I see on a daily basis with my psychic work are looking for their soul mate or a loved one to share their life with, and let's face it, LOVE in its greatest form makes the world go around. If we had love in our lives, I firmly believe there would be no wars in the world and better communication. In feng shui we have cures and space clearing, but I also have some special techniques that I like to give my clients to work with.

## MAKE A LIST

Sit down, light a candle, write down every word of negativity you have ever been given by the people around you, and then tear up the list, bless it, and burn it. Once you have done this, write down all the good things about yourself that you know, or what other people have told you. For some this list may be small, but it is a start and something for you to build on. It is up to you now to believe in yourself, even if you feel nobody else does, and decide what you can and cannot do. Do not forget that it is okay to have boundaries and say 'no' to people that have expectations of you all the time. "NO!" can be very empowering.

## AFFIRMATIONS

Life is something to be cherished and honoured so make the best of it.

To get started with the new you, find out what is important in your life and promise yourself for the next week or so that you will never feel guilty or put blame on yourself for wanting to change the way you live and feel. This should concern yourself and not others. We all have free will and we all need to walk our own true spiritual path. Also, it is good to make contact with the right people that can help you, and often, some of these like-minded people might just want to get involved in some of your projects that may be good for them as well, especially if it is for a good cause. The more of these great people that you find inspiring and resourceful and want to help you, the easier it is for you to move ahead in the world. Remember, never let go of your dreams as they are the driving force for you to create your divine life and live your life to the fullest.

One of the most important keys for eliminating insecurities and establishing a habit of self-love is the use of affirmations. These really work because they raise your vibration, especially when said in front of the mirror because you express them to your eyes, the window of the soul. Affirmations are known as 'food for the soul', and just expressing loving words loudly and clearly reinstates who we want to be in our eyes. Through affirmations we can think ourselves healthy, have a healthy and happy love life, improve toxic relationships by having the confidence to walk away, feel confident, and accomplish everything we ever dreamt about.

Here are a few affirmations that may work for you.

I am a beautiful person and I love you. I AM now ready to meet my soul mate. Every day in every way, I am loved supported and safe. I deserve the best in my relationships and am not afraid to have healthy boundaries. I always find myself in the right place at the right time to receive golden opportunities and meet wonderful people that support me. Every day in every way my life gets better, better and better. I am always grateful for the blessings and wonderful people I have in my life every day. The world is my oyster and I am happy to have the most amazing, loving experiences in my life. I receive openly.

Once used every day, these simple affirmations will become part of your mindset and can never be taken from you. They will open a new reality that you only once dreamt about.

## LETTER TO THE UNIVERSE

Another effective way to reinforce your affirmations in your relationships is by writing them down. Address them to God or the universe, your angels or spirit guides — whomever you want! This act symbolises surrender and trust that your manifestation is now a reality. By making a commitment it becomes even stronger and an investment in yourself.

## ENERGY EXCHANGE

Sharing is caring, and when you give back to the universe there is always a reward. We must remember our friends, our loved ones, and those who are not as fortunate as ourselves. Caring and sharing brings many spiritual rewards and is good karma. I firmly believe that what we give out will always come back tenfold.

## VISUALISE WHAT YOU WANT

Sit quietly in a comfortable position. Breathe in and out three times, and visualise yourself actively letting go of any negativity that you may be holding onto. Think of something you want very much, as long as it is good for your higher self. As you begin to concentrate on what it is you really want, imagine being overjoyed and visualise it happening right now. Hold this for three minutes, and then let it go, surrendering it to the universe.

## VISION BOARDS

Write down exactly what you want in life. I always use a vision board for this and change it every six months. Some people may like to write down their wants and dreams on a piece of paper and put it away for a year or two, it depends on what your expectations are. Often, when you take it out you can see how much your life has changed.

Don't be afraid to expect more of yourself. If it is a partner you are looking for, or a soul mate, make sure you write down exactly what they may look like; right down to the colour of their hair, intelligence, personality, and interests. You need to be very careful with this as it works. You need to know exactly what you want because you might just end up getting it. Vision boards are great to help you achieve your goals in your career, as you are writing down what you want and need in the world. Trust your brain, because the constant reminders, the statements, and affirmations you give your subconscious mind will finally achieve them. Vision boards are really good to have by your desk as they are in a good position to keep it up-to-date. Over time, you will be amazed at what happens and see how you are able to achieve all your wishes and goals. When doing this, always remember to be patient but be ready for the unexpected as anything can happen.

Vision boards are a lot of fun, are generally quite cheap, and do not have to be elaborate. What you use to design your life is entirely up to you. Creating one is probably one of the most valuable visualisation tools available, as they are easy to make and they actually work. I have always been a big fan, and have used them for years because they have proved to me time and time again that they always work, and you will always get results with your goals. As the old saying goes, *the proof is always in the pudding.* They can be plain and simple or incredibly creative and attractive, it depends on the individual. They are a tangible vision of the future, on how you see yourself and where you are going. It is entirely up to you what you create, so long as your intentions are positive and good and you don't hurt anyone.

I always love to stick happy, beautiful pictures of how I would like to see myself in the 'now' on my board, and use happy, quirky quotes to keep me motivated and fill my life full of purpose. Find pictures that represent or symbolise only the experiences, feelings and possessions you want to attract in your life and place them on your board. I use a black texta to write very clearly what I want in the now.

For example, *"I am a renowned spirit medium, successful international author, and have sold out shows wherever I go. I love the work I do with a passion and am truly blessed by spirit."*

Usually, within six months I have to change it as things happen that are now in my life, so I need to go to the next goal.

## MEDITATION

What is the most common thing, besides focus, practice, and perseverance that famous and successful people use in the world today to help them climb the golden career ladder of success? Besides knowing exactly what they want, it is meditation.

By just taking twenty minutes of your day to go within and work on the theta level of your brain, you will feel more energised, younger, and motivated. When you learn to meditate you not only heal yourself as the body needs to rest to regenerate cells, but you can learn to visualise what it is you need in the world. It is also an essential tool to help you discover who you are as an eternal soul and grow spiritually.

It is important for you to see within your heart and connect with your soul's energy to work with those in the spirit world.

You will always be drawn to people and teachers who will help you learn, but at the end of the day it is your own spiritual guide who will, in the long term, show you the way to reach higher vibrations. Earth teachers can only show and teach us so much. This process does get easier, and the technique can be mastered. Daily practice and dedication to meditation are needed to encourage communication with our loving guides, angels, and spirit helpers living in the spirit world so that they will help us on our life journeys.

Meditation is not only a wonderful process for self-discovery, but it is also the key to good health and wellbeing because it brings balance and harmony into our lives. Many successful people in the world meditate and are able to focus clearly and achieve their desired outcomes. By going within and using meditation, you can manifest and create your own reality.

With the energy on the planet now, everything is changing around us as we move into the fifth dimension, or what is called the *Age of Aquarius*. This involves a quickening process, so everything appears to be amplified.

To support this process, we send love, light, and healing to not only ourselves but to everyone we know, and every living thing on the planet. If someone upsets you, either say your piece, or bless him or her and walk away. When you meditate, call on the light to help lift your light body so it will make it energetically easier to go with the new energies coming to the planet now. Daily meditation helps you to ground yourself to these new energies. It is also a time to take charge and be aware of negative thought forms because they can attract negative people or destructive situations if they are not deleted or dealt with.

When you finish your meditation for the day, it is always a good thing to close down your energy by imagining your chakras closing down like little lights. It is also a good thing to send healing, forgiveness, and gratitude and to all the people in your life. This includes your enemies (who are spiritual teachers here to give you the lessons you signed up for before you came here from the spirit world). This will help you move on.

Remember, not everyone will be on your vibrational frequency, so not everyone is going to be your friend.

When we are working in groups, we connect with what is called the *over-soul*. This is a collective group in the spirit world that includes all our guides and higher selves joined together as one. When people leave one of my groups, I will always cut them off from this energy so they are no longer connected to the group metaphysically.

For meditation, find a place where you feel safe, secure, and where no one can interrupt you. You can find and create a place in your home, which would be ideal, a favourite place in nature, or a quiet place where you work and will not be disturbed for a while. Once you have done this, always make a point to try and meditate at the same time every day for better results. When you do this you are making a date with your own guide and spirit helpers. Once a day would suffice, but twice a day would be even better.

## HIGHER SELF

Sometimes in life we have difficulties communicating with our work colleagues, loved ones or just people in general. We are often put in situations in life where it is just about impossible to have a civil conversation because of misunderstandings, confusion, or emotions. Nobody is perfect, and we have all had times in our lives where our emotions rule our intelligence, making it impossible to bring closure to a relationship, get on with the boss or a colleague, or simply move out of a bad relationship.

By talking to the person's higher self telepathically, we can conquer this problem. It is an easy technique that really works. Just by trusting in yourself and talking to the person's higher self, you can bring healing to any situation.

One day, a client came to me with tears streaming down her face. She told me that every day for the past two weeks she was being harassed on her mobile phone. Every time she answered it, there was nothing but silence at the other end. It would ring repeatedly, every day after 5pm, and sometimes up to 20 times. When she answered it, the person would suddenly hang up, leaving her feeling terrified. This put her in a desperate situation as she felt someone was stalking her, and her life was in danger. She found it difficult to sleep at night and became too frightened to be alone or even walk down the street. Her happy disposition had changed dramatically to a person who was desperate, depressed, and full of anxiety.

Connecting to my higher self, intuitively, I felt the perpetrator was a woman. Sitting her down, we determined who she was. The person who came to mind was someone my client remembered as a person she used to work with who had once been the girlfriend of my client's now boyfriend. The other woman was obviously full of jealousy and was taking her revenge out on my client in a nasty and terrible way.

My client was shocked and could not understand how anyone could be so cruel, especially as when they worked together they had always been friends. She herself was a very spiritual and nice person, and would never want to hurt anyone in a malicious way. The ex-girlfriend was obviously hurting and in need of healing so she could move on with her life. Feeling more relaxed now, my client gently closed her eyes and we proceeded with 'The Higher Self Healing'. A dialogue was set up with success and my client was feeling a lot better. That evening the phone calls ceased. The healing was finally complete.

## HIGHER SELF HEALING

Sit in a comfortable position, make sure you have switched off the telephone, and that you will not be disturbed for a while. Close your eyes and gently breathe in and out three times, slowly, relaxing as you let go of any emotions and negativity that may be stored in your mind, spirit, soul, and body.

Feel your loving connection to the source and fill yourself deeply with unconditional love and light. This will make you feel calm, warm, and secure.

Picture an image of a beautiful pink bubble in your mind's eye sitting in front of you. This is a healing bubble. Now put the person you would like to have a dialogue with inside, and then step inside yourself.

Ask them if you have permission to talk to their higher self. A simple 'yes' or 'no' is all you want. When you have their approval, it is now okay to continue. If you do not, keep asking until you do. Now begin the dialogue in a gentle and calm way, stating clearly and precisely in a loving tone exactly what you want to say. Listen for an answer and keep talking to the person until you have reached a conclusion. If there is no conclusion, try for a better outcome next time.

## CUTTING OFF OLD CONTRACTS OR TIES

Often in life, certain people come into our lives to teach us lessons. Once we have learnt these lessons, or *spiritual contracts,* we need to move on, as the relationship can become toxic and create bad chi energy. This exercise is good for cutting off old and worn energy that no longer serves us from the people that are no longer in our lives, or mean us harm. It is good as it helps both parties move on. It can also get rid of negative energy that we may have been carrying towards that person and other people who may be tuning into the old, destructive patterning we carry with us. I have tried this myself and have found results immediately as the karma or contract is finished.

1) Visualise a blue figure eight, with gold in the middle.
2) Put yourself in one side and the other person in the other.
3) Now imagine ties, old ropes or vines wrapping around you from the other person.
4) What colour is the energy on the ties or ropes? Is this energy, thick or thin? How does this energy make you feel?
5) Now cut the ties or ropes off with a sword, knife or a pair of scissors.
6) When you have done this, cut the centre of the figure eight and blow the person away into a big, pink bubble of love. This is your healing bubble or healing room. No harm can come to anyone, as it is a sacred place of love.

7) Once you are there, in your mind's eye, tell them exactly what you think of them. Now, once you have done this, tell them who you are as a person and how you want to be treated in your personal relationships.
8) When you have done this, tell them you love them and forgive them. Tell them the contract you once had is now terminated. Now it is time to bless them, say goodbye, and step out of the healing bubble. Send the healing bubble, full of green healing light, into the source of love.
9) You are now able to move on as the contract is terminated and the person will generally go out of your life. You may hear from them once, or they may try and contact you, but they will also benefit from the healing and move on as well.

## CREATE YOUR OWN STORY

This is your opportunity to be the author and creator of your own show. For this you need to write a story of at least one or two pages in the present tense about your dream situation. This is how you want your life to be. Be very careful what you ask for because you might just get it.

Nowadays, with the new energies coming through and the way energy is moving faster here on this dimension, you will notice your manifestations happening a lot quicker than you anticipated. Always believe in your dreams and don't listen to what other people may say. Of course, some dreams will take a bit more time to manifest, but never give up! You will be pleasantly surprised with what you end up with.

## MANDALA

Every year I create a personal mandala for myself as a reflection of where I am at in my life. It gives me a good look at my relationships. Mandala is a Sanskrit word meaning *circle*. Mandalas are symbols of the universe and its energy. Tibetan monks create the archetypal templates to remind us of the cycle of life and death. A mandala has many layers of meaning, and are used to represent cosmic diagrams and as support for meditation.

Over the last decade, Tibetan art has become a part of the western cultural landscape. Periodically, the Dalai Lama and groups of Tibetan monks travel around the US, conducting healing ceremonies, creating sand mandalas, and performing traditional music and dance to bring attention to the ongoing struggles of Tibetan people worldwide and for the Tibetan independence.

You can create your own personal mandala using colour as your medium and the four elements of nature.

**Water** symbolises love and trust.
The undines or fairy kingdom represents water.

**Earth** is for introspection and transformation.
Earth is where the gnomes, pixies, elves and goblins reside.

**Fire** illuminates and clarifies.
The undines or fairy kingdom represents water.

**Air** gives us knowledge and wisdom.
The butterflies, birds, beetles, and winged creatures represent air.

Find yourself a quiet place, light a candle and play some calming music. Make yourself as comfortable as possible. Now as you prepare and centre yourself, draw a large circle. Using your many coloured pencils or other materials, draw and colour your own symbols or designs inside the circle, on whatever you would like, with relaxed and happy thoughts. Express you, and so whatever comes up, just draw and colour. Remember, this is time for you, so take your time and try not to rush. Now, relax and let your imagination flow, and have fun.

Mandalas are an expression of you; a reflection of your hopes, your dreams, and perhaps ideas of how you see yourself on a spiritual, mental, physical, and emotional level, now, and in the upcoming year.

When you have finished, get somebody else to look at it and see what their impression is, and what they find, or come up with. You will be surprised at how much information comes up about yourself that you may not even be aware of. It is always incredible how spirit can work through us. Mandalas are not only a tool to guide you: they can also remind you of who you are.

# CHAPTER 7

# *Real Life Experiences*

When people ask me what I do for a career, I will often tell them I do many things. As a psychic medium, I do trance work, run séances, rescue lost souls, or what is commonly known as *ghostbusting*, and work with the basic art form and principals of feng shui. People often question my work, which really amuses me. This became quite evident to me when I first opened my office not far from where I live. The real estate agent who leased me the property was quite happy to hear from his sister and mother in the spirit world, and happy for me to feng shui his office with certain cures, but warned me to call myself an 'energy worker' and nothing else as it would upset the small Christian village where we lived.

Everything in the universe, including ourselves, the people around us in our everyday lives, animals, and things around on the planet are made up of pure energy. When this energy gets blocked we have chaos in our lives but we can change all this with cures and remedies on every level with feng shui. There are also two types of energy we can work with.

*Light energy* is loving, warm, and composed of unconditional love. This energy is stronger, healing, protective, and pure chi energy which is the most powerful and strongest energy in the universe.

*Dark energy* is thicker and extremely manipulative, works faster, but is extremely malevolent and, in most cases, has repercussions. For example, people who work with the dark arts, or this type of evil energy, may be successful for a while when they use it but in the long term they will suffer emotionally and will never feel fully loved in their personal relationships. The negative energy that they are working with will always, without question, bounce back to them, according to the universal laws. As the saying goes, *what you throw to others will always be returned.* Often when I am clearing dark energy from clients, their homes, land, or business premises by clearing the clutter, burning sage or dried gum leaves, I will find this energy hard to work with. With time and patience, it will eventually go into the column or portal of light I have brought down from the spirit world.

## STACY'S HOME

When I cleared out my friend Stacy's home, we needed to hire a two-tonne truck to get rid of all the old family treasures they had collected over the years. This had to be done of course when no one was around, as Stacy's family were all really bad hoarders, and it would not have been possible with all the yelling and protests that would have gone on. Most of the stuff was just rubbish now.

Besides being unloved and no longer used, they were piled on top of each other, squashed tightly behind doors, squeezed into hidden corners, and stashed under beds. As for the family garage, that was another story. Stacy had asked the family to help, but only a few items were put in the bin and there were still heaps of things left, especially old toys and shoes under the beds. I was thrilled that Stacy was taking my advice as she had complained for years how she felt stuck and was now finally taking action, surrendering to her inner feelings, and getting rid of all the junk that she had stashed everywhere and had taken over her home. The annoying thing was most of the items she had problems with had sentimental value as they were passed on from family members. Things like old and worn furniture, uninspiring pictures and paintings, cutlery, books, bottles, and kitchen appliances she seemed to be saving for a rainy day.

Once the truck was loaded and the family had arrived back home, the children were all shocked at first but began running around the house, laughing and yelling at each other how different the home felt and how much space they actually had now. Their once tiny home was now bigger, better, and was suddenly transformed into something completely new. Placing a few cures around the home like a water fountain in the *career* section, an elephant with a small quartz crystal on its back and its trunk up facing the door to help her husband work, and moving a few more things around into places for better chi energy, I was exhausted, but said I would come again another day and give more advice once we had discussed what she wanted.

Thrilled to bits at what we had done, she asked me if I could also help support her with the colour consultant she had hired that was going to go through all her clothes. Feeling intuitively that she really needed me with this one as I was sure it was going to be a hell of a task, I agreed, but reluctantly, as I know for a fact that Stacy is one of the biggest collector of clothes and apparel I have ever known. She is always at bargain shops.

After a couple of hours of ruthless nitpicking through Stacy's jam-packed clothes cupboard, I laughed nervously to myself as I watched Stacy squirm nervously and go pale. The ruthless woman started throwing out most of her wardrobe, complaining that most of the clothes were not suited to her colouring, did not only suit her anymore, and were two sizes too small. Stacy nearly died when the woman went on to explain her theory of how Stacy was still trying to live like she was still in her twenties, when it was time for her to move on.

In hindsight, the whole procedure was really good for Stacy. The woman did her an enormous favour as she realised that she was the biggest hoarder of all time and was now free to reinvent herself. After the woman left, I helped Stacy carry all her bags full of precious things over to the Salvation Army bin. Stacy cried for a week, but now there is a new woman emerging to create the life she always wanted, with the new chi energy in her life.

## ROB AND SUSAN

Rob and Susan bought a new home and were excited to start their new lives together. Unfortunately, their dream slowly turned into a nightmare as unbeknownst to them, they had inherited an unwanted energy from the former people that had lived in the home. No sooner had they unpacked everything and moved in, it became difficult for Rob to sleep at night because the master bedroom seemed to have a strange, disturbing energy that made him feel anxious and kept him up all night.

The new home, over time, had the same effect on Susan's small dog. It was sick all the time and refused to sleep or even go in the bedroom. When I checked the home, there were no lost spirits in the house, but the home had a terrible energy they must have inherited from the past owners. When I psychically tuned into the walls of the bedroom I could hear and see angry faces in the walls, and feel in my psychic vision the sound of screaming and violence which made me feel nauseated and sick to the stomach. There were also marks on the door and floor, evidence of some type of past violence where someone must have been banging a heavy object.

Once I worked out what the problem actually was, I told Susan and Rob my thoughts, and horrified, they asked me to fix it straight away as they had no intention of ever sleeping again! They needed their sleep.

Assuring them that everything would be okay, I began to smoke out the room with some sage and gum leaves, clearing out all the negative energy until it was gone. I then lit a red candle and walked around the home, blessing it, and asking it to look after the new owners who promised to love it. The next step was some simple cures like moving the bed away from the door as it was in the *coffin* position. They were both lying with their feet facing the doorway. If this can't be done in your home, then a simple cure would be to place a rose quartz crystal up on the ledge of the doorway. I also suggested some other cures to bring in good chi energy to make them feel that the home was now theirs. Two days later, Rob rang me up and thanked me. Apparently he had the best night's sleep in a long time, and Susan was excited about the new colour plans they had for their new home.

## THE BURNING BED

One day I received a phone call from one of my clients, a businessman I had met at a conference, who had just bought a place in Sydney's eastern suburbs. Larry was a hard-working man in his early fifties who had just relocated from the US. He had his own company, travelled a lot, and was looking forward to living in the new home he had just purchased. He was married to a wonderful woman and they had two children.

As a lifelong intuitive himself, Larry was very interested in the work I did and was keen for me to come and tune into his new home and give it my blessing. He also wanted me to check for any earthbound spirits and negative energy that may have been hanging around. From what I could pick up on the phone, the home sounded very grand and I was excited to see it. Larry sounded as enthusiastic as always, but I could tell by the tone of his voice that something was definitely amiss. Underneath the merriment, my intuition was screaming at me, telling me things were not good at all and that my friend was troubled and unhappy. But I could not quite put my finger on the problem as yet.

When I arrived at Larry's, he welcomed me warmly and invited me into his enormous three-story home. As we sat down in the kitchen, he offered me a coffee and we sat and chatted about what we had both been doing. My sixth sense had been correct about him being out of sorts, I could tell just by watching him tap his foot on the chair leg that he was not his usual self. He seemed troubled and withdrawn and I could see dark rings around his eyes, making me think that perhaps he hadn't been sleeping properly for a few days, or had something heavy hanging on his mind. When I asked him what was wrong, he just shrugged his shoulders and said he didn't know. He was excited by the beautiful new home but this was overshadowed by an uneasiness and anxiety he couldn't explain.

From the moment I stepped onto the property, I did not get a good feeling myself. The house, though very grand on the outside, seemed to me to feel lonely, creepy and sad. It did not feel welcoming at all, and I shuddered and crossed my arms to protect myself when I felt the coldness emanating from the property slip into my consciousness. As soon as I stepped through the front door and into the hallway, the sadness I was sensing became overwhelming and seemed to follow me through into the kitchen where we had our coffee.

This worried me straight away as something wasn't right and it was my job to get to the bottom of it. Keeping my thoughts to myself and not wanting to upset Larry too much with my observations, I finished drinking my coffee and started to scan the home. With Larry at my side, we walked around the home. I felt really bad, because I did not have it in me to say I loved his new home. The whole house made me feel uneasy and it was obvious my first impressions were right. The house had an odd feeling; weird and unwelcoming. Larry, who had gone quiet, must have already picked up on what I was feeling and just followed me sheepishly, waiting to see what I said. It did not take me long to work out the problem because as soon as I stepped into the master bedroom, the energy became thick, dense, and extremely depressing. Scanning the room, I could sense straight away there were definitely no earthbound spirits in the home but there was a lot of dark, negative energy, especially in the spot where Larry and his wife slept. Without saying much, I silently opened myself up. I began to psychically pick up the sounds of screaming and yelling coming from implanted memory in the walls.

When I told Larry what I had heard, he looked at me dumbfounded for a while.

Then he admitted that I was correct, as the couple he had bought the house from, as far as he could work out, must have always been fighting. Larry told me the man had been nearly impossible to make a deal with, and his wife was always yelling in the background whenever Larry's solicitor had spoken to them on the phone in the days during the exchange of contracts. When it came the time for them to sign, the man was aggressive and unpleasant to deal with. My intuition told me this problem was most certainly left behind by the last owners. The energy we were experiencing was their negative residue. I could not help but wonder how Larry managed to sleep in the room at all as I nearly doubled over with the effects of the toxic energy.

I have seen this time and time again, and I always encourage people to clear the energy in their new homes as soon as they move in, so as not to be affected by the energy of the former inhabitants. The most effective way of doing this is by clearing the home of old energies by smudging with sage leaves. Larry must have picked up my thoughts because, without me having to say a word, he began to blurt out all the problems he was having since his family moved in. He complained that he and his wife kept arguing and could not agree on anything. In the meantime, she had returned to the States to visit her sick mother and had taken the children with her. Before she left, she had moved into another bedroom on the far side of the house and they had not been speaking. He was heartbroken and did not know what to do to fix the relationship. He said he loved his wife very much and could not believe how everything had suddenly become so bad. I told Larry not to worry and reassured him the problem was easy to fix, but it was up to him, on his wife's return to get his marriage in order.

"Don't worry, Larry, everything is going to be all right," I said, gently patting his back. "Something very bad has gone on here before you came along, most probably before you even bought the house. I can also pick up that there was a lot of violence in this room because I can hear crying and screaming from the walls. The old energy is still here in the room. It will take me a while to clear it, but once I do my job, you will love this beautiful old home."

Not knowing what to say, Larry just stared at me blankly, a look of complete misery on his usual businesslike mask. I could not help but think how sensitive this man really was and how much he must really love his wife.

"It is no bloody wonder everything went crazy," Larry said. "As soon as Lizzie and I moved in with the kids, we have not been able to stop fighting. We don't even talk anymore." Looking around, he started to cry again, wiping his tears away. "I just want everything to go back to how it was before we even lived in this horrible place," he sniffed, taking out a hanky and loudly blowing his nose.

"I will try and get you out of this mess by getting rid of the energy, but the rest is up to you," I replied, quite determined to make the situation right. "After all, this is my work and I will do my best to make it all good again."

"Thank you, Kerrie," he said softly. "I knew you were the right person to help."

When I 'sweep' a house, by tuning into its energy, the home will often talk to me so I can pick up on the vibration. I have also found that if you have trouble selling a house, all you have to do is 'talk' to the house and it will tell you everything you need to know. You need to thank your home for looking after you, but talk to it and be firm that you do want to leave. Let the house know in a loving way that some nice people will come and buy it after you and will enjoy living there. This strategy always works for me.

Standing in Larry's bedroom, I brought down the white light, which is pure, loving energy, and wrapped it around myself for protection. As soon as I did this, I could sense the full impact of the dark energy in the room. It felt sad, lonely, and extremely cold. My guide told me what I already knew, that it had manifested from the last couple that had owned the house. My guide went on to confirm my first impression that it was playing havoc with Larry's relationship with his wife and was hell-bent on destroying the love between them.

Saying a prayer, I brought down a beacon of pure, loving light and, in my mind, made a portal in the ceiling of the room. This was opened to activate the release of the ugly energy in the room that was causing all the problems. By doing this, I could energetically push all the old energy out through the portal, where it would be sent off for healing and transmutation. Once this was done, I would flood the room with healing light then

I would close the vortex of energy and finish the clearing by burning some sage, just to make sure all the negative residues were gone, once and for all. As I made the vortex of light, I commanded in the name of God that any evil or black energy that had been trapped in the room should leave immediately.

As I loudly chanted the Lord's Prayer, Larry watched silently as the energy weaved its way up into the vortex of light and disappeared. The left over energy, which would not go into the light, was sent into the earth, where I grounded it deep into mother Gaia in the earth's core.

Evil, dark or thick, black energy will often be impossible to send into white loving energy so it is best grounded back into the earth for the nature spirits to heal. In my experience so far, dark energy is thicker and colder than loving white energy. It is sinister and malevolent, and feeds on cruelty, fear, and violence. You can feel it where there have been murders or wherever there has been violence, such as suicides or aggression of any description. No matter how many times I come across this energy, I find it is still frightening to work with as it is pure evil and feeds on people's fear. As most of the energy passed into the vortex, I could psychically still hear crying and shouting, which made me want to shiver. Soon, all the dark energy had drained from the room. When I had finished, I lit more grandfather sage, and started to sweep the room again with the smoke. Placing the smouldering sage in a bowl, I continued to sweep the room, even wafting the smoke inside cupboards and wardrobes where negative energy might have been trapped or be in hiding. When I finished cleansing the room, I placed the bowl of smoking sage very carefully in the middle of the bed so it could gently keep burning until the energy in the room was completely clear. This would ensure the smoke has enough time to do its work. As I did this, I told Larry we should quickly check the other rooms again, just to make sure everything was fine. As far as I was concerned, the bowl with the sage would be safe and by the time we got back everything would be back to normal again. Walking around the rest of the house I double-checked all the rooms, making sure everything felt good by scanning each room with my third eye and checking in with my guides.

After I had finished, I stood chatting to Larry in the hallway telling him everything was looking good. He seemed pleased and more relaxed now, and told me he was glad of my help and could not wait to get things back into order. I also suggested some quick feng shui tips to add to his *career* and *relationship* section of the home that would improve relationships generally. I suggested rearranging the furniture to improve the energy as well. He laughed when I said this and explained that his wife had suggested the same thing before she took off to the States. As we made our way back to the master bedroom on the other side of the house, we could both see thick, grey smoke coming out of the room. Horrified, Larry and I looked at each other and ran back into the room, now full of suffocating smoke. Somehow, the glass bowl in which the sage stick had been slowly burning exploded and burst into flames, the embers landing on the sheets and blankets on the bed.

Screaming, we quickly opened the windows and grabbed the burning bedding and threw it outside, where it landed on the lawn below. Then we both ran outside and grabbed the hose and put out the fire that, unbelievably, continued to burn. In all my years of clearing houses and offices and working with sage, I have only twice experienced anything like that before. Not knowing what to say, we both looked at each other and started to laugh hysterically. We must have carried on laughing our heads off for a good 20 minutes or so before we could stop and catch our breath. The whole thing seemed extremely funny. Larry may have lost some sheets and blankets but, at the end of the day, the bedroom was undamaged. He was convinced he had just saved his marriage.

After we had finished rolling around the ground laughing, I apologised and offered to pay for the damaged blankets and sheets, which were now strewn across the yard. Larry refused to take any money and kept thanking me for everything I had done. I made a mental note to never take my eyes off burning sage again.

A few days later, I received a phone call from Larry who told me that things had settled down and the house was now much more in order. Even better, his wife called to say that she missed him too much and she had come back early. She was back in his bed and was thrilled with the new sheets and bedroom apparel he had bought her. He sounded like his old self again and kept thanking me for everything I had done. He also said he had just been promoted in his company and had finally gained the position he had been hoping for. He said there were no more arguments and the whole family was happy now to enjoy life in their new home. Not every event has such a happy ending but spirit works in so many mysterious ways. That's why I try always to keep an open mind and expect the unexpected.

## MARGO'S NEW HOME

Margo is a wonderful woman I know who is a successful feng shui consultant. She is an expert in her field, in both corporate and ordinary suburban homes, but whenever she has a difficult case where she suspects there may be more than stuck energy in the space she is working in and lost souls are involved, she will always ring me and ask me to finish the job before she completes each project. Mind you, this does not happen a lot, but you would be surprised how these lost souls or unwanted spirits can cause havoc in the home and create imbalance to a space, making it chaotic for any single person living there.

After many successful years in the industry, Margo always knows when she needs the extra help so will always call in an expert, namely me, as she knows that the feng shui will never work until the medium has done the rescue.

After moving back to Sydney from Western Australia, Margo and her husband bought a new home near the water to settle into. At first they were over the moon and could not believe their luck, but it did not take too long before the family felt and sensed a weird presence there, almost as if someone was watching them all the time. The other thing that bugged her as well was a terrible, sickly old smell that kept lingering around certain areas of the home, and the weird thing was, no matter how hard she cleaned and scrubbed certain areas of the home, it would always come back again. Also, unexplainable things seemed to go wrong all the time and all the batteries in her clocks and homewares kept going flat for no explainable reason. Before too long, she realised that the older home had more of a history than the family had bargained for, and exhausting all her attempts to make things right, she finally gave me a ring and asked if I would check out the home and clear it of any unwanted energies or lost spirits.

Margo had a pretty good history of what I did as she had worked with me on several cases in the past when she lived in Sydney, and some of her clients had similar problems. The whole concept of lost spirits in the home and especially her own, God forbid, absolutely terrified her, but she was determined to get to the bottom of her problems. If she did have an unwelcomed visitor it was going to go. Finally realising she had a real problem on her hands, she rang me and begged me to come as soon as possible as the whole scenario was driving her crazy and she was finding it hard to settle. Her husband was having problems with his job and it was difficult to sleep at night because of the sound of heavy, loud footsteps outside the bedroom. The weird thing was, each time they got up to investigate there was nothing there.

No sooner had I arrived and walked through the front door, I was suddenly overcome by a terrible, nauseating smell that hit the back of my nose and somehow travelled to the back of my mouth, right down to my solar plexus making me feel sick and nauseated like I was going to vomit. This awful smell hit me like a tonne of bricks and I could not help but feel I was swimming in a sea of human excretion.

Holding my nose and jumping back, I immediately was taken aback when I saw an elderly spirit gentleman sitting on a chair, right at home, as if nothing in the world even bothered him. Not believing my eyes as he was so vivid, I had to laugh, as he was just as shocked as me when he realised that I could sense and see him as well. This must have given him a bit of a fright as I sensed a morbid look of contention on his face. He must have been wondering what was I doing there and was even more confused that I could even see him. After a while, I pulled myself together as the whole thing had given me a shock, and I asked him his name.

Telling me his name was John, the spirit man told me that he had built the home himself, had lived there for many years, and remembered being sick, but not much else. It was easy for me to see from the many cases I had done that like most earthbound spirits he was confused, as he kept asking where his wife was. When I repeated this to Margo, she informed me that the man who built the house was a conveyancer and had built houses in his former work. He was also called John but he had died many years ago, quite suddenly of a heart attack.

After his death, the family and young widow stayed for many years until all the children had married and moved on. Not wanting to live alone any longer, his wife sold the home to Margo and explained how the family had many years of happiness, but she felt it was finally time to move on as there were too many memories. She could still feel her husband around most of the time. Once we had established who the spirit man was, I gently told him he was dead, bought down a beautiful white light and told him to move on to the spirit world, as his time on earth had finished. No sooner had he disappeared, the whole room shifted to a warmer temperature with all evidence of the smell gone.

The next day, Margo rang me up and said how the energy in the home felt a lot better, there had been no heavy footsteps in the middle of the night, and her husband had exclaimed happily how the horrible smell had disappeared. Not long after, Margo's husband got a new job with more money and the family now absolutely loves their new home.

## THE STORY OF FREDERICK

Frederick had been married to his wife Anna for a very long time. They were both well-educated and came to Australia from an overseas country when they were young. Frederick was able to get work straight away and was very successful. Anna, unfortunately, was not. Instead, she became despondent and developed a type of depression which later turned into schizophrenia. Her whole personality changed and she not only became housebound, but mean and unhappy, and she made everybody's life miserable.

Frederick rang me and asked if I could clear his house. Anna had been dead for some time and he could feel that her energy was still around. He had moved on and had a new woman in his life but things were starting to disappear from his house, and he was sure that it was his wife, who he feared was not happy about his new arrangement. He was convinced that his wife had come back to haunt him, and was jealous and angry that he was in love with another woman.

As soon as I arrived, I encased the house with a purple and gold bubble of light to make sure if there were any lost spirits in the house, it would be impossible for them to escape once I got there. Walking in the front door, I felt the presence of his wife sitting on the lounge next to her husband. I could feel she had difficulty breathing when she died and she showed me in my mind's eye what had happened to her.

When she was sick her husband took her to the hospital. This was the first time she had left her home as she had been housebound and sick for so long. She later died at the hospital and was terrified, so instead of leaving with her spirit guide and crossing over into the light, she decided to go back home and jumped back into the car with her husband. She went on to tell me that since her illness she was terrified of leaving the house and spent most of her time in her bed.

Her husband, who nodded in agreement when I told him what she said, later confirmed this. Walking into her bedroom, I saw her lying under the covers in her bed where she spent most of her time. The energy in the room was not only toxic but very heavy, sad, and depressing, and I don't know how her husband still managed to sleep there of a night. Moving gently closer, so not to scare her, I brought down a porthole of light and told her to open her eyes, that she was dead and no longer belonged here, and it was now time to cross over and go home where all her loved ones were waiting for her.

Once I explained that her loved ones were waiting for her, and that it was time for her to leave, she willingly seemed to go, jumped very swiftly into the light and said goodbye. This made me realise that she was ready, because sometimes if lost souls are really scared, you can hear them whimpering. You have to talk to them very lovingly and gently to coax them to leave. I knew that she was happy to go because she had such a miserable and lonely life. Before she left, she asked me if I would tell both her husband and her daughter that she loved them, and she was sorry for all the pain that she had caused.

As soon as she was gone, I cleansed her room with grandfather sage and energetically cleared out all the stale and negative energy from the rest of the house that had gathered in all the years of her illness. I also instructed Frederick to sage the house for seven days as a precaution as he was terrified that she would come back, even though I reassured him that would not be the case. Then I went to all the doorways of the house and sealed the energy with some special oil I had made up, which consisted of olive oil, garlic and sage. This stops or acts as a deterrent for any other unwanted spirits or negative influences coming in.

After doing this, the house felt very calm and relaxed for probably the first time in ages, as all the old energy that had saturated the house for years had finally shifted into portholes of light I had set up energetically in the corners of the rooms. I suggested to Frederick that he may think of getting rid of Anna's things, as she had been passed for a few years now and clearing a lot of the clutter he had stored everywhere would be good. When he was ready, I could come back again and help him with some useful feng shui cures. Saying goodbye, I hugged my client warmly and wished him a long and good life. Smiling happily, he waved goodbye and closed the door behind him.

## MARCELLA, THE SAD AND LONELY WIDOW

Bill and I had been working together clearing houses, doing feng shui, and spirit rescue for years. Our working life started at a spiritual church many years ago, and we became friends when I ran a circle for up-and-coming mediums that wanted to work in the industry and who belonged to the church.

Spirit rescue is not an easy job, so we joined forces when spirit kept sending me more and more of this kind of work. My role as a medium is to speak to the spirit in question and to help it cross over as these types of earthbound spirits are generally very confused, in some cases fearful, and do not understand that they are *actually* dead. Once my guides and I have found the lost soul, which in many cases is often hiding somewhere in the property, I talk to it gently, explaining that it is dead, ask it to open its eyes and tell it to cross as its loved ones are waiting on the other side in the spirit world. I can also do this work remotely over the phone and do so with interstate clients or homes and properties all over the place.

Bill's role is to assist with all the immense energy we need to help the spirit cross, to set up a vortex of pure light energy for the spirit to leave in, and clear up any fractured or negative energy from the two worlds that have unnaturally blended and collapsed together with the presence of the lost soul.

By using a dowsing rod he is able to indicate any residue or blocked energy that may be left behind once the spirit has crossed. After we have finished he mops up the residue energy and clears the space, bringing it back to balance with dried sage. This procedure will also smoke out any other lost soul or spirit that may be hiding and that we have not found while doing our scan of the properly.

I always say that the good things in life are free, so I encourage people to use our native Australian gum leaves when smoking, but dry them first, as it is a great remedy to clear away negative energy stuck in a home. By doing this we are clearing the negative energy, clearing any phenomena, and what we call 'balancing the room'. Once smudged and cleared of blocked and gritty energy from the lost spirit, the room will realign or balance again and all the negative energy will simply lift. Sometimes, we may have to do the smoking thing a few times as we find on some occasions, not only does it not weaken the lost soul but the spirit in question will hide if it does not want to go into the energy vortex, so we have to keep smoking them out till they will cross. On some occasions, if the job was too big or difficult, we would often ask another medium to come along for the extra help and assistance, as sometimes you need a lot of energy to do the job, but generally we preferred to work by ourselves. If the client still has problems I ask them to ring me after a week when things have settled down.

It is an incredible responsibility to do this work, with many highs and lows if you decide to take it on. It can also be a heavy burden and you have to have your wits about you to do the work. There are also, sadly a lot of non-believers in the world that expect us, as working mediums to prove ourselves all the time and are quite happy to tear you apart with ridicule, if you let them, even in this day and age. At the end of the day, unless you have experienced some type of phenomena or had a reading with a loved one from spirit come through, I suppose it is difficult to understand what this is all about. That is why I am always trying to educate people to make them understand that there is indeed a spirit world and we have many angels and spirit helpers that are here to help us on earth in every way they can. We just have to learn to trust, have faith and know that we are not alone; our loved ones are always with us on the other side. Sure they have many things to do in the spirit world, but they will always lend a helping hand as they are connected to us through their love, which is eternal.

Most people think that these things only happen in the movies and it is not real, but I am here to tell you about my world. They also think you will find a ghost in old abandoned home in the middle of nowhere for that matter, which is really not true and quite ridiculous, as I have always said that you will always find lost souls around people and busy places, like hospitals, shopping centres, sports centres or where there are lots of people, as they are attracted to us and need our energy like parasites. Other spirits will just follow you home for whatever reason, and every situation we come across is never the same.

The work of a medium and energy worker is always a different experience, no matter how many years you have had, as you never know who, or what, situation is going to present itself when it walks through your door. Sometimes it makes me feel as if I am back at the hospital, in the good old days, working in the casualty ward as you never know what's going to happen, no matter how many years you have been doing the job, or what you think you may know.

Marcella was an old acquaintance of Bill's wife. As we drove out to her property, Bill told me how his wife's friend was from the same village back in her old country. Marcella was a widow and had lived with her son until his death twelve months earlier from cancer. After the death of the son, the woman kept telling anyone who would listen that her house was now haunted, and she was convinced that her son's spirit was unhappily trapped on the earth plane, because the phenomena was increasing in duration at a rapid rate. She was now terrified to go to sleep at night. Every time she got up to investigate, all the noises would stop and there would be an eerie, dull quietness as if nothing had happened. She also told Bill that the heavy, loud footsteps she was experiencing were now becoming more frequent, and seemed to be not only outside her bedroom window, but outside her bedroom door and next to her bed. She also complained that she had felt something very strange one night while trying to sleep, like a cold, heavy pressing feeling on her head. After that terrifying incident, she became too scared to lie in the dark, and had gotten into the habit of keeping the light on next to her bed, which seemed to help for some reason, but it was uncomfortable and hard to get proper sleep with the light in her eyes all night.

Once we arrived at the house, Bill rung the doorbell, quite a few times for several minutes, but never got an answer. Things never seem to go right when we clear houses and properties, so this did not surprise me at all, I just sighed and went along with it. After what seemed like a good twenty minutes or so, we both began to think it was getting ridiculous, so I asked Bill to check the address again and to give her another ring to see where she was and if anything had happened. The woman knew we were coming as Bill told me he had spoken to her as soon as he got off the phone from me, the day before, but all I could think was that I had other places to be, and I was starting to get a bit impatient. The burning sun did not help matters as it was one of those days where it was really hot and it was starting to burn my skin. Looking around desperately for a bit of shade, with sweat running down my face, I started to feel miserable, as there was nothing but concrete and small little pots scattered everywhere.

Thinking Bill had made a mistake with the address, I asked him to ring the woman again to see if we were in the right place. This must have gotten things moving because as soon as he did this, the front door suddenly opened and a large middle-aged woman appeared out of nowhere, a look of worry on her beautiful face. She seemed pleasant enough but still eyed us off suspiciously before asking us to come in. After Bill had a few words with her, she welcomed us in and apologised several times for not answering the door more promptly. She explained that she had heard us at the door, but was busy trying to lock her dog up so he would not disturb us while we worked.

Happy to finally get out of the heat, I started to wish I had stayed outside because as I stepped inside the woman's house, all I could see was a whole collection of toxic clutter blocking the hallway, which included a large collection of papers, clothes, rubbish, bits and pieces, and stuffed boxes as far as the eye could see. The poor woman must have been a hoarder, and it was no wonder considering the stress she must have been going through over the years. One can only assume these sort of things, but it got even worse as we stepped in further. To my dismay there were lines and lines of junk, and mountains of things all piled up on top of each other. It was everywhere.

Stress and grief can do many things to a person's mind, so it was easy to see we had more than one problem to deal with that day. Making a mental note to address the matter after we cleared the house, I smiled sweetly and followed Bill into the living room, which was the same, but if there is one thing I cannot tolerate more than an unwelcomed ghost, it is a cluttered home. Clutter, no matter what, in any shape or form is toxic and will always upset and block the natural chi energy in the home, which in turn creates disharmony and imbalance, and if you think about it, how can anyone that wants to have a healthy and happy life, even think to want to live this way with so much waste and rubbish everywhere.

It always amazes me to this day, the way people really live in their homes, as it always tells me a story, and can be quite different from when you first meet them at work, socially, or your first impressions. This is because I often have memories come flooding back of my earlier days when I was a community sister, working for the state government in Norway. In those days, I really loved my work as I was always going into people's homes to check on and see all my patients, instead of the main hospital. It was a wonderful experience as all my patients were very kind and were extremely grateful to have me help them. The other great experience I am extremely grateful for is that I learnt trust my senses and instincts at such an early age, as they would always be on full alert going into uncharted territories as one never knows what to expect.

The one thing I always remembered were the smells, sounds, feelings, and the impressions I got from the patient's surroundings, as it would always give me a clear indication on how the person was coping, mentally, physically, and emotionally in their daily lives and in the healing process. For example, if they had a modest clean home which they took pride in and were able to manage, or had people helping them, it would always indicate to me that they were doing well, were happy and their life was probably in order. If it was an unkempt, dirty home, with toxic clutter everywhere and smelt of unpleasant odours, then more than likely they had quite a few problems going on that they were not telling me about and needed extra help with.

To me, our home is the foundation and a base for us in our busy lives. It is also a place for us to enjoy with loved ones, friendships, family and pets. It is also a sacred space to recharge our mind, body and soul, so we can prepare ourselves for the many challenges and life's experiences that come our way from what is often, sadly, a very hostile world. When you work with feng shui, it is amazing how much a space, home, property or dwelling where someone lives can give you a bigger picture of their life.

Once we had settled into the living room, the woman introduced herself politely as Marcella. She must have been in her late sixties, with deep, haunted, and sad lines of gloom and worry etched deeply on her ragged face. She was also dressed all in black; a symbol of mourning and a way of showing deep respect for her loved ones in death. From her deep accent,

I could hear that she was definitely from somewhere in the Balkans, because her accent was very strong and hard to understand at times, but her vivid description of what was going on was very helpful, as it was clear and easy to understand. The thing that I did not like though, was the obvious total chaos and mess around me as it was all built up in some type of pile, right up to the ceiling, making it hard to move and get around.

Within minutes of sitting down on a chair, I started to sense very strong paranormal activity in the room as everything suddenly became very cold and all the hairs on my arms were sticking straight up. I was starting to get a creepy impression that we were no longer alone. We had some spirit guests and were being carefully watched by invisible eyes. Then suddenly, before I had a chance to say anything, out of nowhere, a vase flew past my head, missing it by inches, and landed with a loud crash on the ground before me. *Poltergeist*. I sighed. Just what we needed.

Screaming loudly, poor Marcella jumped to her feet and started crying hysterically, grabbed my arm and begged me to make it all stop as she was terrified, had enough, and thought she was going mad. Apparently, from what she kept telling us, this type of thing was going on all the time. I was definitely some type of spirit trying to get nothing but attention. Assuring her that we were there to help, she began to calm down and was happy to hear us say that by the time we left, everything would be okay and she would have nothing to worry about ever again.

Opening myself psychically, I slowly stood up, asked the spirit or spirits to come closer. I began to hear the rumblings of a very angry male spirit talking gibberish in my ear. With so much energy in the room I began to burp very loudly and I felt my solar plexus energy centre open straight away, as the spirit energy grew closer. When I asked the spirit what it wanted, the male energy told me in no uncertain words to shut up and get out of his house. As soon as this was said, I could feel the spirit draw even closer and felt a great coldness of cold invisible air, pushing me back down in the chair. Not worried, I screamed back at the spirit to back off, stood up again and pulled down extra protection of light, asking my guide and angel helpers for extra assistance.

Once I had done this, I told the spirit man in no uncertain terms that he was not welcome here, it was not his world and that he was dead, and had to leave straight away. All he had to do was open his eyes and look for the light which Bill had set up as a vortex and porthole of light in the corner of the room. This must have been confusing for our unwelcomed spirit guest, because it took a while before he answered again.

After a long silence, the spirit man, who was very persistent, began to speak to me again, complaining that he did not know the woman living in his house and wanted her gone, not him. Before I had the chance to answer, I felt the spirit man come too close for comfort and felt a freezing cold hand on my head and my ears began to buzz loudly. Telling the spirit to back off again, we commanded the spirit man into the vortex of light and within seconds he was gone. Once he had crossed over I felt his presence again and was able to communicate with him properly.

The lost and confused soul was a spirit man called Alex, and he was from Germany when he was alive. He said that he lived in the house all alone and built it with his own hands and was very proud of it. When I asked him why he had not crossed when he died, he became silent again and could only remember going to sleep in his bed.

Like most earthbound spirits, he was totally confused for a long time but was grateful now that we had come to, what he understood, help him. He knew on one level that things were not right, but kept trying to get the woman's attention by moving things around all the time because he was disturbed by the dog that barked all the time. Once he had said these few words, within minutes the whole energy of the room changed and it began to feel tingly and warm again, indicating to Bill and I that the room was now clear.

Testing that all was well again, Bill pulled out his dowsing wand which spun around nicely, indicating that the room was clear. Why the spirit man had not crossed when he died was down to his own free will. I can only assume that he did not understand that he was actually dead, as everything still seemed the same except for the woman walking around his house.

Sometimes, when we do the spirit rescue, the spirit has more of an understanding that they are dead once they have crossed over. Occasionally, they will come back and say a few words before they explore their other life waiting for them in the spirit world. Other spirits will just go and never return, unless of course they are visiting loved ones.

Once we cleared the main living room, we proceeded to clear the rest of the house before reaching the son's room. Once there, the awful gnawing feeling in my gut from earlier was correct, because there was definitely another spirit living in the boy's room, but this time, hiding in the cupboard. This spirit was a much younger man that appeared to be in his early twenties. When I asked who the spirit was I heard a tiny voice say that he was scared, that he was called Peter, and that he was Marcella's son. This information gave Bill and me quite a shock and for a few seconds, we felt very sick and shaken. As you can imagine, it was so terribly sad.

Marcella had been correct all along, so we called her in and explained the situation, and then asked her to help us cross him over, as he had no place here any longer. Bill explained that earthbound spirits interfere too much with the energy on our plane, as they interfere with the dimensional shift and energy of the two worlds, causing imbalance as if it was in time warp.

Why Peter stayed I cannot say for sure, I can only assume why he did, but one thing was certain; he would have been confused, sad and miserable, living in a very dense and dark grey world, with no existence but that of a thin shadow, not able to communicate with anyone, eat, have a proper life, and worse still, be unable to feel any love or warmness. Also, him being there would only interfere with his own soul's progression and karma for reincarnation and his future lives.

Joining hands, the three of us said the Lord's Prayer and asked Peter to step into the light to go home, where his loved ones were waiting for him in the spirit world. The good thing was, Marcella totally understood that Peter had to cross. In fact, it was her own mother's love that helped her son cross to where he would be met and looked after by his relatives and loved ones in Spirit. Once we had finished, Marcella started crying and hugged both Bill and I as she knew now her whole life was about to change, and both she and her son would be able to finally heal. Her worst nightmare was now over. She was no longer afraid and finally understood why there was so much craziness and paranormal activity in her home.

As I said before, why the minority of souls stay and become lost is always the question, but I can only assume Peter did not want to leave his mother alone, as they were so close when he was alive, according to Bill's wife who knew the whole family. In hindsight this was not a good choice, as the poor boy was stuck on the astral plane and was probably very lonely.

For those who do not know, I have been told by many spirits that I have spoken to over the years who live in the spirit world, that it is indeed a vast consciousness, full of light and love and wonder. To some it may look like a magnificent city but to others a place of nature. I am also told that everyone looks younger, once they have crossed the veil, and the energy is warm, brighter and incredibly more loving than planet earth. Peter, now free, and back home in the spirit world, will be able to visit many horizons of incredible splendour and beauty. Once he has visited the spirit hospital, he will be able to visit his mother anytime he likes, and he will now be able to *feel*. The cold grey world he was living in was no man's land, and it was imperative that he should cross over and heal. After a couple of goes, and a lot of coaxing and convincing, he finally went, and the energy quickly turned warm again in the once cold room.

Walking through and scanning the energy in the rest of the house, very thoroughly, so not to miss anything, Bill and I managed to cross over two more confused and earthbound spirits that for some reason were stuck in the home and needed rescuing as well. This meant looking under beds, opening cupboards and looking into the ceiling of the roof, as often the spirits who know we are coming will try and hide, as they are afraid of someone like me who knows they are there. Gradually, by the time we had finished the whole house, which funnily enough looked rather small from the outside, I could suddenly feel all of my energy being drained from my body. I was now feeling very tired and extremely weary.

It never ceases to amaze me how much energy is needed to do this type of dimensional work, and no matter how many of these cases I have worked on over the years, I still felt the same. Nothing has changed. Any type of energy work you do can be draining, so it is no wonder I make it a daily routine to work out at the gym, meditate, and take care of myself with my diet, as this work is so extremely taxing on the body. If I were not in the best of health, I would not be able to work at my highest potential and would not have the energy I have to do this type of work.

I remember once talking to one of my teachers from the US, and he said that it was extremely important to be very fit to do any type of spirit or inter dimensional work, as the energy can sometimes be heavy and energy depleting as we are using so much of our own core energy in the process. We also need to keep our minds stress-free and have a good, balanced life so we are able to channel the energies successfully from spirit for the clearing work we do.

Once Bill and I had finally finished the whole house and all the small rooms in the place, I turned to see Marcella standing behind me with a puzzled, strange expression on her face. Asking if she was okay, she nodded with a little smile and said very softly that she was glad she was not going out of her mind with all the weirdness that had been going on for months, but was still trying to digest what had happened right in front of her of her as we worked.

When I asked her very politely about the clutter and told her it had to go, she said she never used to be like that. She was always neat and tidy in the past, but the grief had really gotten to her. She explained, very sadly, that it had happened after the death of her son as she felt she had lost control of her life because of the incredible sadness, grief and shock at losing all her family. She had thought about getting help but was worried because of her language deficiencies. Grabbing my hand with gratitude, she wiped tears of relief from her eyes, and sighed. She was so drained, she had felt it for years from all the weirdness going on, as when she tried to explain it to others she was embarrassed. She was scared people would think she was mad. She also said jokingly, that she would not in a million years believe it really existed until she experienced it herself.

Once we had stopped working, the unexplainable, tingling sensation that she had felt, which seemed to race up and down her body when the spirit passed over, suddenly stopped as soon as the clearing had finished. This to her was confirmation that something was going on, even though she did not understand it, as once she had said the spirit had passed, the feeling went away. Feeling elated, she wanted nothing more but to sit and chat and asked us to stay and have a cup of tea and some sandwiches. I could explain to her how to clear and feng shui her home, as she needed a new start as she had lived in misery for so long.

It sounded like a good idea at the time, as I was starving and needed to replenish my energy before the drive home. Also, it would give me an opportunity to sit and talk to her about all the clutter. If she was serious, she had to do this first before I gave her certain cures to get her life really going.

Her little dog, Sammy, who had been locked up in the laundry, must have sensed it was his time to come out, and hearing our laughter, started to bark loudly, demanding to be let out. Happy to have the dog's company, I assured the widow that her little dog could join us, as I am a great animal lover myself and have several cats. No sooner had I said this, Marcella laughed and raced to open the back door to let her little friend in. Before too long, the little dog started to run wildly around the house, barking happily and licking everyone, while we all laughed and welcomed him to join us.

A couple of months later Marcella gave me a ring. At first I was not sure who it was, but then I remembered her soft, crisp Baltic accent. She was chatting excitedly, like a happy little girl in my ear. It was a lovely surprise to hear from her again and I was happy to help her in any way I could. When I asked her how she was going, I could sense by her voice that things had improved greatly as she could not stop laughing, and was delighted to tell me how she had hired a skip and got rid of most of the rubbish that she and her husband had collected over the years.

She also could not agree more what a difference it had made once she had cleared up the mess for her and her beloved dog Sammy, as they now had more space and she could finally find things that had been lost for years. If anything, I felt she was definitely back again and more at peace now. I was also thrilled when she said she felt her son around at times and was convinced he was happy now and with his father in the spirit world, because a song they had both loved would play loudly on the radio out of nowhere, or she would have very clear dreams where she saw him smiling and running in fields of wild flowers. In the morning when she woke up, her pillow would be damp from tears of happiness where she must have been crying in her sleep. She kept saying how relieved she was to know that her family was safe and being looked after. She was also relieved the angry spirit had left as he was such a nuisance with his moving things around all the time and making such a commotion. Laughing again, Marcella said she would never have believed any of it, if it hadn't happened to her.

## JUDY THE HAIRDRESSER

One day I received a phone call from a woman called Judy. She and her partner owned a hair business in the city, but too many things started to go wrong when they moved their premises to a new building. Judy sounded upset and asked me whether I could investigate what was going on in her new studio as she had never experienced anything like it before. She was also interested in me doing some feng shui, as it was impossible to catch up with the money she was making before and she was desperate for me to activate her *wealth* section. Apparently, she was having some type of ongoing paranormal problems all the time and they were really starting to bother her and the young girls she worked with. They had all started to freak out.

I was extremely busy with work and said I would not be able to get to her house for at least a week. The spirit world has its own agenda for me as I was already fully booked and seemed to be doing a lot of houses and offices at the time.

As I sat and listened to her worried voice, I asked her for a moment of silence so I could tune into her home over the phone. I quickly made a pretty good assessment of the situation. I could see the overall problem wasn't too bad and ensured her that she was safe and gave her the usual instructions and protocol for similar problems. I told her that by tuning into the energy over the phone, she probably just had a few pesky spirits that wanted her attention, and again assured her there was nothing to worry about.

About a week later, my partner Bill and I finally arrived at the studio and we found a lost spirit in the middle of the room that I had already sensed over the phone. Before too long we found more spirits that were hiding in cupboards that were just as lost and confused. From what I could understand, the girls must have inherited the spirits from the building when they moved in, and as it was in an old area of Sydney, this is very common.

After we finished scanning and clearing Judy's place of work, which everyone commented was feeling lovely for the first time, she said she had another problem which she had not mentioned earlier on the phone. This was another building on the property where her brother worked, and he wanted us to come and clear his space as well. Once I activated the wealth section of the studio, which looked pretty good to me anyway, Bill and I said we had time and would have a look. The funny thing is, when she asked me to do this I had a feeling that we would be doing two properties that day because when I originally scanned the space over the phone and listened to her voice, I was seeing two spaces in my mind, with two problems.

The brother's office was on the other side of the property and quite a walk from the hair studio. Judy told us that he was a lovely guy, that they were close, and he worked as a printer in a couple of rooms he had hired in a large old building. As soon as Bill and I stepped into Mike's printing firm, we could tell this was going to be a big job because the energy in the room was dark, cold, and depressing, and evident of paranormal activity. The whole atmosphere was dull and miserable, so I added extra protection of white light around myself before I proceeded to open up. When I had opened up myself psychically, Bill and I sensed a strong spirit presence enter the room. Tuning into the spirit's energy, I heard the voice of a female spirit talking in my ear who told me that she had died in a fire, and that there were others there that needed our help. The spirit woman said that she thought her name was Faye when she was alive. She appeared confused and disorientated to me, but she understood that on some level she did not belong in this world. Apparently, from what we could work out, there had been a massive fire years ago that had killed quite a few people as they were trapped and could not get out. They must have known that Bill and I were coming because we could sense the energy of many more that started to gather in the room. The spirit world has ways of helping their own, so Bill and I were happy to help in any way we could. When we relayed the message to Judy's brother, he started to cry and said he could feel the sadness in the rooms all the time, and could not understand what it was.

After we finished the job, we went back to Judy's studio and she caught us up on what she knew. Apparently, the property was once a halfway house many years ago where some violent people had once lived. The rumor was they had lit a fire that killed many innocent people in the home when they could not get out. The newspapers said that the people who had died, probably died of smoke asphyxiation but we will never know. Mike, Judy's brother, had somehow, being a sensitive man, inherited this negative and sad energy, and all the confused, lost souls when he moved in years later. The whole saga hadn't helped his business or his personal life as he had become depressed over time. He was deeply affected by all the negative, haunting energy there. Both Judy and Mike were extremely grateful to Bill and me for our work and clearing, and kept thanking us for all the time we spent, but we were both happy that the brother and sister were finally able to find peace and harmony.

## TOM AND JEFF'S FLOWER SHOP

Tom and Jeff were a lovely couple that owned an older building in the city that was used for their garden business. From the moment they moved in, they had ongoing problems and were convinced their building was unlucky and full of some type of bad energy. No matter how hard they tried to get their business going nothing worked, which was unusual as all the other businesses around them were highly profitable, always busy, and people always seemed to be around, but for some strange reason, never went into their place. After great expectations of a wonderful business and spending a bit of money hiring a feng shui specialist from China, everything seemed to go well for a while, but within a year the business went down again and nothing they did or tried seemed to help to improve the energy. In the end they gave up their dream and put the business on the market. Frustrated, they called me as a last resort to try and get the business going so they could sell.

Once there, I could not help but notice the work of the master feng shui expert, but sadly, I could see that this was not working because of the paranormal energy that was hitting me in my stomach. It was starting to smell in my nose and I could feel it in my other senses. The whole space was very heavy, dark, and obviously had a haunting that that was causing all the problems in the business. His cures, though very insightful, were unfortunately blocked because of the paranormal energy.

After walking around and clearing the heavy energy as I went, sending it off into portholes of light, I finally made my way down to the basement of the building and before too long, I found the real reason for the blocks. Huddled together in a tiny cupboard in a trapdoor in a wall, were five wretched lost souls that had been burnt and killed in a terrible fire that had destroyed the building many years ago.

For some incredible reason that I don't know, they had not passed over to the spirit world when they died, and were trapped and terrified in a time warp. When I told the boys what I had found, they just stared at me in disbelief and said they remembered that the older building had apparently been an old boarding home in its heyday, but had been rebuilt after a terrible fire that seemed to destroy most of the main structure.

When they told me, this I became overcome with incredible emotion and started to cry like a child as I could feel the wretched agony, pain, and horror which these poor innocent souls must have suffered. Once I got myself together, I sniffed loudly and wiped my face, all blotchy from the black, runny mascara, and muttered the Lord's Prayer under my breath as a tribute to the dead spirits to send them on their way to the spirit world for healing.

Within seconds, the whole room suddenly lit up like a Christmas tree and began to fill with an amazing, bright light, full of what seemed like a thousand or so healing angels, all singing and reaching out to the spirits to take them home. After what seemed like a long a few minutes, we all stood back, stunned, and watched in disbelief as the heavy, depressing energy that had lingered for so long disappeared without a trace.

Within two months of the spirit rescue, Tom rang me up, thanked me a thousand times over the phone, and happily informed me that the building had sold for the exact money they had hoped for. They were over the moon and delighted by this, as Jeff being a Queenslander, did not want to stay in Sydney anyway. His mum was getting older and he was sick of all the cold weather. Tom, tired of the stress was happy to follow him and looked forward to their new adventure.

## THE VENGEFUL EX

Ingrid was a lovely client of mine who ran her own beauty business. She had been a client for many years, and I first met her when I helped her get her business going with some simple feng shui tips. Everything went well for her in the business, most of the time, but whenever she had an argument with her ex-husband, who was very violent and never seemed to leave her alone, she would break up with her then boyfriend and the business would, for some strange reason, go down again.

When she was small, she had been very close to her grand-mother who was well-known in the small village she came from. Her grandmother was called Anna, and she was a wise woman who was able to heal people with her herbs and hands, but Ingrid had not seen her for many years, as she did not want to come to Australia and begin a new life here. This made her sad as the family was very close, but they managed to stay in contact with the old woman until she died, through pictures sent by mail and the telephone.

As she was very open and psychic herself, inheriting her abilities from her grandmother, Ingrid had always been interested in anything she could get her hands on of a supernatural nature, and was always reading books and doing different classes in her spare time. She believed in her heart that her grandmother was now her guardian angel, and was looking after her.

A couple of months later, Ingrid rang me, extremely upset, and said she had heard through family and friends that her ex-husband had been killed in a terrible car crash overseas. That same night when she heard the horrific news, she was visited by what she could only describe as a very malevolent, dark, and sinister force that psychically attacked her by pressing her down in her bed by her head and trying to strangle her, leaving marks on her neck. Screaming for help to her grandmother in spirit and asking the angels from the light as well, the dark force gradually disintegrated and disappeared back to wherever it had first come from. Remembering what I had taught her when I first cleared her office and home, she quickly saged both premises again as his tormented energy seemed to be following her everywhere. Crying hysterically and not understanding why this was happening to her, she begged me to come as soon as I could, as she was frightened to death and felt like she was going to have a nervous breakdown.

No sooner had I arrived at her rooms, that I could sense there was definitely a spirit in the premises as all my senses were suddenly on full alert. Walking slowly around the place and checking every space, I was shocked and mortified to find the cowardly spirit of her ex-husband hiding sneakily in one of the cupboards at the back of the business.

Not wasting anytime and quite angry at what I had seen, I quickly told him he was dead, his time on earth was over, and he needed to cross so he could heal all his wounds and be with his loved ones in the spirit world. After sending him off in a column of light, with the help of the angels and my own guides, I told him he was not allowed to come back as Ingrid needed to move on with her own life. Ingrid started crying and told him to go as well. She also told him that she was sorry for the way things had ended up and wished him no harm. Within seconds of this, the whole room suddenly changed and everything became warmer and lighter again. Overjoyed with happiness, Ingrid hugged me and said she was glad the whole saga was over. Now she could get her business up and running again, and it was finally safe to meet someone.

Humanity, as we know it, is so full of many joyous and wonderful moments in life. Luckily for us, good will always prevails over evil, and if we live our lives according to the universal laws, if we love ourselves and one another, have faith in spirit and never feel a want to harm anyone, things will be good. Life is often about lessons and learning and with an open heart, our journey will always be easier when we learn to forgive others who have hurt us, so we can then move on in our own journey on planet earth. Very sadly, not everyone in life will want to be our friend as life is full of petty things like jealousy, envy, hatred, and judgement. We would have to be naive to think that we were all the same.

One thing I have learnt in the lessons of life is the law of attraction; what you give out, you will always get back. People who constantly work with negativity or the dark forces will always have unhappy lives, and any negative energy they give out, will always come back to them tenfold. If you chose to live a simple, uncluttered life and move on from your problems, you will be able to live the life you want, as without a doubt, positive energy will be in your life, just like you create in feng shui.

## JOE'S FACTORY

Bill, my partner in spirit rescue, had an elderly friend called Joe who owned a factory in the far west of Sydney. Joe was having problems selling his business. The place had been on the market on and off for a couple of years, and seemed impossible to sell no matter what Joe did. It presented well enough, but every time Joe thought he had a potential buyer, something would happen out of the blue and the buyer would pull out at the last minute with no explanation. Joe had no idea why this would happen as the business was doing well, but he was becoming more and more disheartened, as the years marched on. As far as he was concerned, the place had to be haunted, needed a good space clearing, and he was also open to creating some good chi. He had run out of reasonable explanations why things went haywire every time he tried to put the business on the market.

Even though Joe was a very religious man and a devout Catholic, he had known my friend Bill for years and the work we did, so it did not take him long to figure out that perhaps his place could be haunted. Too many things were going wrong that he could not account for, and often when he was alone and working late into the night, he would hear muffled voices and strange noises coming from inside the building, like people talking in the distance, as well as weird pungent smells like sewerage, and loud banging sounds that seemed to come from nowhere.

Joe found these events very unsettling and so did his workers. It caused him huge problems with a high staff turnover, and those who stayed refused to work back because of all the strange goings-on. The other odd thing was that no matter how hard they tried to warm the place, there was always a chill in the air, even on the hottest of days.

Every time Joe tried to investigate these strange events, he would never find anything. Another ongoing problem was the electrical circuitry in the office. Even though it had been repaired many times over and brand new equipment installed, they experienced ongoing lighting and electricity problems. Lights were going on and off, and machines turned themselves off for no apparent reason whatsoever.

Everyone used to joke that a ghost must have been playing tricks on them and old Joe, but it was long past the point of being funny. Every time Joe put the business on the market, all hell would break loose and either everybody would be at each other's throats or someone would get injured in the yard. Joe was worried that one day one of the frequent accidents would be serious and someone would end up dead, a possibility he wanted to avoid at all costs. He was fed up and just wanted out. The daily stress of running the business was starting to take its toll on his health. His dream of retiring seemed to become more and more distant, and he was considering closing the doors and going bankrupt. Then, just when he thought things had hit rock bottom, his eldest son Peter, who managed the business, walked out and took a large share of the profits with him. Joe was devastated and found it hard to imagine why his own son would do this to him. Broken-hearted, it was now up to Joe to pull the business together and make one more attempt at selling it.

When Bill explained what was going on, I realised that we would have our work cut out for us, and wondered if Joe expected us to create some type of miracle that would save the day. Hearing his story, I did feel for him and wondered how difficult it would be to help clear Joe's myriad of problems. I remotely tuned into the factory's energy and intuitively sensed earthbound spirits running rampant. I could also sense much sorrow emanating from the space as well. According to Joe, he had bought the property at a bargain price years ago and I could see why. It was obvious the previous people were having problems as well, and just wanted things to calm down so they could get on with their lives.

Poor Joe inherited the mess when he bought the business over 20 years ago. He was now paying heavily for his mistake and probably wishing he had never set sight on it. Bill and I could certainly help him with the energy in the factory and deal with any earthbound spirits that may have been causing havoc, but when it came to his son, that would have to be a matter he would have to deal with. Whatever karma they had between them was solely up to them to work out. Greed and power are lower vibrations that certain people carry with them. According to Bill, Joe's only son must have had heaps of this energy but it was not our job to judge. We were just there to clean up the mess energetically. When the day finally came to do the job, fate was on our side as it was a beautiful, crisp winter morning without a cloud in the sky.

We decided to drive down together to Joe's yard, as it was about two hours out of the city, and it would be a good time to have a laugh and just generally catch up with things. It is not that often that we get a chance to talk, as when we do see each other we are either working, or sitting in a meditation and trance group together with other mediums. I always enjoy Bill's company, as he is an interesting, amusing fellow who has travelled all over the world. He's a good source of information and always has a good yarn to tell. He has done a lot of work with earth energy and dowsing, and is a master of his craft. He has a wealth of knowledge that he freely shares when I work with him. As I am always a keen student, always wanting to know more, it helps me with my own work, which is being of service to spirit. Even though we are very different people, we complement each other in our work. It is usually my job to contact the earthbound spirit and convince it to cross over. Bill's role is to help with its release by sending the spirit healing. We do this by telling the spirit to open its eyes and look into the light, and to make sure it realises it is dead and does not belong on the earth anymore. Bill's job is to back me up and make sure the spirit crosses over. Sometimes we may need to spend time coaxing them. Once we have done this we close down the portal of light, and cleanse and clear the remaining area.

Mischievous, dark or malevolent spirits are another story entirely. They are different to ordinary earthbound spirits, which are usually quite easy to cross over, as they are merely lost and confused. Dark, menacing energy, on the other hand, is harder to work with as it does not want to be crossed over at all, is defiant, and likes to lurk in the shadows and cause havoc to people they may come across. I once removed an ugly octopus type of dark energy off a friend, a light-worker, who was working full-time with drug addicts in the city. He said he felt something creepy just attach itself to him after working late one night. He was rundown at the time and not looking after himself, so his psychic protection was very low. That made him an easy target for psychic attack and this awful force attached itself to his energy field.

Satanists also work with this type of dark negative energy, as it is thicker to feel, full of ego and power, and works generally faster than white light energy that is pure love. I can only describe it as pure evil, full of misery and pure hatred, and it is known to make people feel depressed, suicidal and sad. People who work with the dark forces often have dreadful lives as there is virtually no love whatsoever in their lives. Their emotions are full of ego, loathing, greed and fear. This trickster energy also feels dirty and sticky and takes a long time to remove, as it is stubborn and vengeful. I have felt a mass of this type of energy where there have been violent crime cases, murders, and sometimes suicide incidents, and I am sure there is much more out there, like pedophile rings that harm innocent children, something which hope I will never experience in this lifetime. This energy goes hand in hand with the people who commit terrible crimes that harm others. Unfortunately, this energy has been around from the beginning of time and has brought much destruction to the world we live in. Two mediums working together are pretty hard for these to resist, as our combined energy is stronger. The dark forces will then be swept up by the powerful white light energy of pure unconditional love and cross over to the healing hospital on the other side.

After we have finished helping the spirit cross over or completing the rescue, we continue to work together, scanning, repairing, releasing, and clearing unbalanced energy still trapped in the room. Often when you have a ghost, lost souls or any type of negative energy that has built up over time in any area or space, you will have an imbalance in the natural energy and flow of that area. There may be energy tears, cracks or breaks that can cause havoc as two different dimensions are in play. This is easily brought back into harmony using white light and prayer. The reason I work in a pair is for back-up, as you never know what is going to happen on the day as the work can be extremely draining and, at times, challenging. On the odd occasion when I have gone out on a job by myself to release more than a few earthbound spirits it can sometimes take forever to send them into the light and I find I am depleted of energy for the next few days. Nothing bad has ever happened when I have worked alone, as I am always with my trusted guides. However, you never can tell when working with unseen forces and paranormal activity, as no experience is ever the same.

After driving for about an hour, we finally came to a large intersection and stopped at a red light. As soon as I hit the brakes and the car came to a halt, two very large black crows that had been sitting on a telegraph pole on the side of the road suddenly swooped over the car and landed with a bang on the bonnet. Gasping, both Bill and I looked at each other and laughed loudly. Funny little things like that always happen on these jobs and this day was no exception. Bill and I sat there dumbstruck, as the larger of the crows squawked loudly at the windscreen, demanding our attention and flapping its great, outstretched wings. Jumping up and down on the bonnet, the crow kept making a hell of a racket, as if berating us or trying to tell us something. Meanwhile, the smaller bird just stared at us boldly through the windscreen with its large yellow eyes. It also seemed to be doing a little dance as well, but not as aggressively as the bigger bird, which seemed like it wanted to peck out our eyes.

The crow is believed to be the shapeshifter of the bird world, and from my own experience I believe they symbolise ancient magic. Some say that their magical qualities include prophecy, skill and knowledge. The ancient Celts believed them to be an omen of death and conflict, in the Middle Ages they were said to be sorcerers and witches, and the crow's foot symbol was used to cast death spells. It is easy to believe this after a visit to the Tower of London, in England, as the crows there are enormous and look rather ominous, probably more because of the place's cruel history and the wretched energy that still lingers to this day.

Along with the owl family, crows are one of my favorite birds, as they are fascinating, highly intelligent and can be taught to communicate with humans. When they are around, I know they are always watching me as they love to gossip. They are mischievous and like to steal shiny items, but are also suspicious and shy. I have a family of crows, a mother and her offspring, that have lived in my garden for years. I often give them a treat of cat food which they love and think is delicious. Quite often, they will sit quietly and wait until Harry, the younger and least bright of my feline threesome, has nearly finished his supper. They will cleverly distract him for a second and when he turns his head, they will quickly gobble up all his food.

Another screech from the bonnet brought me sharply back to reality. Now, all I could think about was how to explain the scratches from the crows on the car when I got home. If I told him about the birds, he would probably think I was making some type of excuse up and taking the mickey out of him. He would never go for the crow story anyway, so I decided that it might be best just to say nothing.

As soon as the light turned green again and the car started moving, the crows took off within seconds and disappeared out of sight. Once we had passed the traffic lights, I pulled up on the side of the road, jumped out of the car and held my breath as I checked the car for any signs of scratches on the bonnet. Luckily for me there wasn't a single mark, so there would be no explaining to do when I got home. What a relief. Laughing loudly, Bill and I drove on, amused at the goings on.

Our day was turning out to be quite an interesting one and, if there was one thing I was pretty sure of, we'd find two earth-bound spirits waiting for us when we got to the property. Strange things often happen to us on the way to a job, such as being abused by someone on the road or occasionally my navigational system is affected and plays havoc, sending me all over the place, or other inexplicable delays. Why this happens I have no idea but I see these events or delays as little signposts from the spirit with whom I will be doing rescue work on the day. Regardless, I always protect myself with white light before I do this type of work. That way, whatever happens, I know I am always safe.

Crows are also associated with shamanistic healing and 'crow medicine', which to me, is messages or omens. In the case of Joe's property, they were both. The birds were clearly telling me that there was negative energy to be removed, and lost souls that had to be rescued.

As soon as we found the factory and drove onto the property, Joe, who must have been waiting for us, greeted us with open arms. He seemed pleasant and friendly enough on first impression but on closer inspection I could see he looked old beyond his years, as if he was carrying the whole world with all its problems on his shoulders. As he laughed nervously and shook my hand repeatedly, I could sense from the way he carried himself that he was indeed going through a rough time. With a cigarette sticking out of the side of his mouth and dark circles under his eyes, I could see that he hadn't had much sleep lately, and was going through some really serious stuff.

Moving into the factory, Bill and I quickly protected ourselves with white light, grounded ourselves and opened up psychically as we carefully scanned and checked each room, one by one. I knew there were two earthbound spirits, to rescue.

In the entrance to the building, I felt a chill that seemed to travel up my legs and made me shiver. As soon as I called out, clutching a cross I wore around my neck, and asked if anyone was there, I heard a male voice. He identified himself as Tom Simpson and said he had lived on the land before it was used as a factory. He said he had no idea why he was there, didn't even know that he was dead and was quite happy to leave. Calming the spirit down, I reassured Tom that it was time to go. I explained to him that he was dead and his loved ones were all waiting for him on the other side. All he had to do was open his eyes and he would see a brilliant white light that would help him cross over. As soon as Bill and I opened the portal of light, we felt an overpowering amount of pure loving energy come flooding in and sweeping the room. No sooner had we done this, the spirit man disappeared into the blinding light, without so much as another word or any sign of struggle. I'm sure he was probably quite relieved to go, as are most lost souls.

Soon after Tom departed, we sensed a second spirit that was in hiding. When I called out and asked if anyone was there, I immediately felt a deep sadness descend on me like a heavy weight and a ghostly male voice answered, telling me his name was Edward. I asked what he was doing there but, commonly for earthbound spirits, he said he had no idea. He told me he had worked in the factory when it was first built which, according to Joe, was over 60 years ago. He had died when he suffered a heart attack but he had not crossed over, possibly as he was agitated and frightened. Without wasting any time, Bill stepped in and we opened another portal of light for the spirit man to leave. Within seconds the spirit man's guide must have stepped in to help him leave as he just vanished. His years of imprisonment, isolation, and confusion were over at last and he was free to move on in spirit and meet up with the rest of his loved ones on the other side. Both of these rescues were the easiest we have ever done. It was obvious they just wanted to go home. As soon as we healed and cleared the office space, the atmosphere seemed to expand energetically.

Lost souls that have not passed over when they have died on any property or in a space can manifest in problems with electricity, drainage, health issues, emotional problems, or some type of paranormal interference that cannot be explained. Earthbound spirits and blocked chi, the natural energy in a space, in a building or on a property, will always be affected. When we related this to Joe, he had no idea of who these men had been. After our discussion with Joe, who was now becoming more and more fascinated with our work when he witnessed it first-hand for himself, we decided to go further into the property and see if there was any more blocked energy besides the two trapped souls we had just rescued. As Bill pulled out his dowsing rod, I began to follow him around, feeling for areas with dark, negative and blocked energy, using my legs, that often worked in a similar fashion to dowsing rods.

We detected a couple of pockets of dark energy in the main centre of the building, which we cleared and unblocked, then applied a feng shui cure. This took a good hour or so as the energy was denser and harder to dispatch. It must have been there for a long time as it was quite stagnant, prickly cold, and depressing. We were given no explanation why this energy was there. Our job can sometimes be very overwhelming and we have to just trust that spirit is working through us as we send the trapped energy into the higher realms for healing and transmutation.

After we finished working on the whole factory for a good couple of hours (it was quite large), we could sense a new energy beginning to manifest that felt lighter and more vibrant.

All the negative and dark energy was finally gone. It was incredible the difference the clearing had made, and even Joe could feel it — it was so much lighter. Pouring us a cup of tea, Joe sat with us and chatted, apparently eager to know more about what we did and excited that things would change now that we had re-aligned the energy. If anything, we had certainly opened up his mind to other things that go on in the universe. We couldn't give him all the answers to everything he wanted to know, as we could only give him what we knew ourselves, but assured him over time he would notice the difference.

At the time of writing, Joe is well and truly back on his way to getting his business in order again.

## DEMONS AND THE ANGRY TRUCKING COMPANY

One day Bill and I were called out to a busy trucking company on the outskirts of Newcastle. The owners, brothers Jerry and Tony, had been having ongoing trouble within their business since they had moved into the new premises only a year ago. Their once profitable company was slowly, for some inexplicable reason, beginning to be ripped apart by the seams due to continual squabbles and ongoing strife. No matter how hard they tried to rectify the problems that presented themselves on a daily basis, everything always ended up in chaos and stress. Not only did they have to sack disgruntled workers, but freight kept disappearing, and unhappy employees who had once worked together in harmony vandalised trucks.

Before the company had moved to the new premises, the hard-working brothers had been extremely prosperous, and able to retain a solid business of happy and reliable workers who had been with them for years. The move was intended to be an expansion for growth within the business but things unfortunately did not go to plan. Ever since the move, everything that they had built was slowly deteriorating before their eyes. It was heartbreaking for the brothers, as you could imagine, and the stress caused many sticky problems. As things went downhill, Tony became ill from the daily grind of stress and left the company. He landed in hospital with severe mental exhaustion and the company was left to his brother Jerry, and his wife, Maureen, to run.

Fed up with all the drama and crazy goings-on, Maureen called us in to see if we could help or give any insight. She had heard about our work, was a big believer of feng shui herself, and was desperate to get the business back on track as everything the family had built for years was slowly turning into a nightmare. Maureen was beginning to suspect that there was not an earthly cause.

A sensible down-to-earth woman, Maureen was also open to the spirit world, even though she said it scared her, as she had heard many stories from her sister, who was also a medium. In a hushed voice so as not to alert her husband, she revealed her suspicion there was something sinister going on within the walls of the building. Not only did she feel sick and drained of energy each time she went to the office to do the paperwork, but also she felt watched by invisible eyes. She dreaded walking into the place as she felt like she was walking into a wall of darkness. She could not shake off the feeling of the negative energy, which gave her goose bumps. She was also fed up with all the bad luck, arguments, and differences of opinions that seemed to be causing havoc. She had known many of the workers for a long time and to witness their aggressive behaviour really upset her. Nothing made sense and she could also see the stress and mayhem it was creating. When Tony ended up in hospital she knew she had to get help.

By the time she called us in she was at her wits end and convinced the place was haunted in the worst way and felt afraid of the malevolent energies at work in the new premises. She was also brokenhearted that her once healthy and robust guard dog had suddenly died from a mysterious illness.

Other mysterious occurrences were going on such as paperwork being moved around in the office from where she had left it the night before and strange noises coming from nowhere when nobody else was around. Maureen knew a bit about energy from what her sister had told her and she had studied feng shui for a couple of years. She had tried to clear the energy herself on several occasions and had some success for a while, but it did not take long before the bad feelings would suddenly return and creepy things would start up again. Maureen knew she was way out of her depth, as she was not trained in getting rid of earthbound spirits and what she called 'demonic energy'.

At first she thought it was her imagination but continuing problems with the electricity, plumbing and sewerage were really starting to get her down. She also complained of certain areas in the place that made shivers run down her spine. Now, she was so scared that she made a point of just staying in her office.

When we drove up to the business, it did not take long to get the full picture of what was going on. I felt the vibes were like a toxic wall of vile energy. It was hard to believe anyone could work in a place like that without feeling affected on some level. No wonder Maureen was frightened and frustrated. Whatever direction I walked in, I was overwhelmed by wave after wave of smelly, unpleasant energy that washed over me. It felt as if a thick, cold blanket of soot and sadness was laying over the property's foundation and suffocating the building and its inhabitants.

As soon as Bill and I stepped out of the car, Maureen came running out of the office looking strained and upset. She was chain-smoking and I felt she was on the edge of collapse. Her husband, Jerry, stood silently in the background and stared at us, looking suspicious and angry. He appeared agitated and refused to make eye contact. Maureen rushed over, apologising for her husband's behaviour and explained he had sacked more staff. They had been dismissed that day but they had gathered outside the gates in protest and he was about to call in security.

In a way I was relieved not to have to talk to Jerry, except to say hello, as he already had enough on his plate and it was clear that he had no understanding of what we were going to do and how we were going to help him. He looked like he was going to explode or have a nervous breakdown. His battle with his staff was starting to take its toll on his health but I could also see he was not going to give up the business he had worked so hard to build. I knew it would be a hard case to work on but I was not expecting to deal with a mutiny as well.

We had been told that the business premises would be closed for the afternoon. We explained that we did not want anyone there while we were working, but nothing ever works out how you think it will when you are working with spirit. It was no surprise either that an angry motorist, which is always a good indication trouble is ahead, tried to run us off the road on the way, as this sometimes happens when dealing with lost souls that do not want to cross over or a really bad haunting where there may be demonic energy involved.

Bill and I felt like we had landed in a war zone but this made us even more determined to get to the bottom of things. Meanwhile, I could feel my spirit guides moving closer, protecting and preparing me for whatever I had to do next. With spirit's help and divine intervention, we would clear the energy once and for all, no matter how long it took. Any lost souls or toxic negative energy would be sent up into a portal of light for healing.

As Bill and I walked around the yard and the office, looking for lost souls and trapped energy, we made a point to stay way out of Jerry's way. Everything that Maureen had described on the phone was starting to hit right into my senses and I started to feel sick all over. As we made our way into certain areas in the premises, my stomach ached and I started to burp. The air was thick and offensive with a cold pungent kick to it that made me want to vomit. At the same time, it almost felt as if a knife had been plunged into my stomach and was being pressed right into my energy centre. No matter how hard I tried to protect myself, I could still feel the pain. Whatever was there was certainly putting up quite a battle and must have known that we were there to send them off.

As the energy began to build up, Bill and I called in more white light as extra protection. Whatever was there did not like the fact that it was being detected, as the energy was extremely volatile. That did not bother us, though, as we both knew that white light energy, which is unconditional love, is much stronger than the dark forces and always wins in the end.

Wrapping white light around myself, I tried to ignore Jerry and the angry yelling outside. As I tuned into the foul energy, I could sense it was beginning to thicken rapidly in one of the rooms. As soon as I started to call out, asking if there were any spirits present, I heard a male spirit voice answer back from an empty toilet block. Our skin crawled as we felt the malevolent presence. As we raced towards the spirit voice, the whole building was in darkness as the electricity cut out. Turning on our torches inside the toilet block, I instantly felt spirit activity present as coldness washed over me and I heard the male spirit voice calling out, asking me who I was. Adjusting my eyes to the darkness, I saw a shadow in the corner, the spirit of an old man. I could sense that he was actually just confused and rather scared, like most lost souls we work with. He told me his name was Jim, and he had no idea where he was and what was going on. I explained that he was dead and he needed to cross over into the light, so he could be healed and meet with his loved ones on the other side.

Telling him to open his eyes, both Bill and I called down a beacon of light right next to him. Without having to ask him too many times to leave, he disappeared without another word. As soon as he disappeared, any negative residue from his trapped spirit disappeared as well and the room seemed to become lighter. Moving further into the other rooms, we came across two other lost souls. Like the first, they were easy to rescue as they were totally confused and had no idea where they were either and so were happy to leave. Again, as soon as they vanished into the light, the dark energy shifted and the room started to become more settled and peaceful. The reason why these souls became trapped there was not given. Sometimes spirit will not give a reason for certain happenings and we must accept this. As mediums, our work is to do our job and get on with it, and not ask why.

After about an hour, everything seemed to finally settle, according to the plan. The old black energy, which once pervaded the whole property, was slowly lifting. When we went back and spoke to Maureen, she became excited and elated, and commented on how different the place was beginning to feel.

Just as we were about to close down and finish for the day, as we were both beginning to feel quite tired and drained, we came across another spirit that was completely different to the other three. This spirit looked like what I can only describe as an old biker. He was more sinister looking than the others and felt aggressive and more menacing. When we told the spirit to leave, it just stared at us and said nothing and we could see it had no intention of leaving willingly. That entity seemed almost demonic, probably due to the drugs it was using while on the earth plane. It was no wonder the place was in total chaos.

Finally, after using angelic intervention, the menacing entity was sent straight over into the light. I am sure there is a place for all types in heaven and the spirit man, once safely there would see the error of his ways and understand his lessons when he stood before his spiritual council and learned what his contract was as an immortal soul.

As soon as we released the last spirit, smoked the place with grandfather sage and sent white light throughout the building via a portal of light, we prayed for the release of any other spirits that may have been present and trapped in the building. It was no wonder the place was falling apart. There was enough spirit activity in the place to sink a ship. There was also an open portal, or crack in the dimensional energy of the building, that had to be repaired. Once we sewed it together with white light, everything would come back into balance. Pouring extra white light into the crack, we finally sealed the energy, poured salt on the ground to cleanse the area, and then felt everything start to calm down.

When we finally finished our work and closed down, Bill asked Maureen who the previous owners were. With a funny look on her face, she remembered that the building itself was once a notorious club and hangout for drunks and drug addicts. She said it was rumoured that people sometimes disappeared on the property, and that heavy drugs were sold and other illegal activities went on there. The council had stepped in and closed the place down because of the violence, and as such, Maureen and her husband were able to buy it at a really good price. Whatever had gone on in the premises can be left to the imagination. As far as Bill and I were concerned, it was none of our business and we had no further interest in knowing.

I would not be surprised if something really terrible happened there, such as a few murders, as I felt so much suffering and pain going on within the walls. That energy was causing all the imbalances for the new owners and workers. Only time could heal the rift that had torn the business apart and turned it into a war zone.

When we left we gave Maureen instructions to continue smoke the place with sage for at least a week, just as a precaution, to help clear any residual negative energy.

About three months later, Maureen rang Bill to thank us for the clearing and the feng shui. She was delighted with the results and could not believe the difference the clearing had made. If anyone there was a non-believer, they had certainly changed their minds as everything was now running incredibly smoothly. She told Bill she had to pinch herself to know it was not all a dream, and how incredible it was to think that they had once had terrible problems.

Jerry's brother was now back on his feet and new staff had been hired. The electrical system settled down and business in general started to pick up. It was as if the place had been given a new lease on life with all the toxic spirit energy gone. Everyone agreed the place had been given the green light and the cobwebs from the past were cleaned away. The one month inspection was never requested, and Bill and I were happy to have had the experience, as every job we do is a lesson. We are always amazed how wonderful spirit is as a teacher. With a bit of faith and good old-fashioned spirit intervention, miracles do happen in the world today.

# CHAPTER EIGHT

## Commonly Asked Questions

1) *Will I have problems if I live in a cul-de-sac?*

   Living in a cul-de-sac can be challenging as the energy from the entire street can accumulate and have nowhere to go. A green and red bagua with a small mirror in the middle can be hung at the front of home to deflect some of the energy, but beware, these mirrors emit a very strong energy which you are directing to your neighbours. Some feng shui practitioners do not recommend these mirrors because it can cause trouble with neighbours, but that hasn't been my experience. In fact, I have used them to stop aggression from neighbours with great success. All I did was place one on the wall facing them and all the trouble went away. You can also use a barrier in front of your home or a wind chime near the front door to handle negative energy. Good barriers include trees, hedges, walls, or screens.

2) *What can I do if I have heavy industrial wires hanging low in front of my home?*

   I always use the magical yellow and black Bagua with the mirror in the middle to reflect busy and interfering energy.

Always hang your Bagua at the front of the entrance to the home, so to reflect any interfering energy back to where it has come from, and remember, never hang your mirror inside the home.

3) *Will I have problems if I live near a T-section?*

I once had a client that lived directly in front of a T-section. This caused many disturbances in the home, as there was an imbalance in the energy. To rectify this, I placed a red and green mirror on the porch of the home facing outwards to reflect any collective energy, and placed a small wind chime on the side to help eradicate the flow of unnecessary built up energy collecting in her home from other neighbours.

4) *What if I have a sloped back yard? Is this negative energy? What cures to you have with feng shui?*

Sloping backyards in the home can present some challenges. It is undesirable as it is believed the land formation carries everything away from the home including good luck, wealth and prosperity. The sloping away allows anything coming to you through the back entrance to be carried off and downhill. Logically, this is also very bad for drainage, as heavy rain will carry away the earth that supports your home, creating mudslides and erosion of the earth supporting the foundations of the home.

To correct this, a retaining wall and back filling the yard can be done to create a significant alteration of the backyard sloping.

Feng shui tips include planting a row of trees that is the same height as your roof to help raise the chi energy, installing a spotlight on the ground so it shines up to the roof, creating direct chi to your home and lifting the energy, or the placement of a large rock at the point where your yard begins to slope to create the illusion of a mountain supporting your backyard

5) *If I paint my front door red will I create more prosperity in my life?*

Years ago when I first started getting interested in feng shui, one of my teachers talked about the importance of the front door as it is known as the *mouth* of the house. The front door is where energy enters the home, which is why it's important to use your front door, and not the door through the garage or the back door. The front door not only brings energy into your home, it also brings opportunity. If you only use your side door and you have money issues, start using your front door and see if your situation changes.

The colour of your front door is very important as it transforms the energy entering your home. My teacher suggested I paint my front door a shade of red to attract wealth. Once I persuaded my husband to do this we were both rewarded within three months; my husband was given a promotion with his work, I opened a successful business, and my daughter's marks improved at school.

A red door is not recommended for everyone. In fact, a red door can cause harm in *north-west* facing home. Different colours are recommended for doors that face a particular direction. If you stand at your front door with a compass and look directly outside, the direction the compass is facing is your *facing direction*. *North* facing houses can paint their front door white, black or blue. Houses that face *west* and *north-west* are advised to paint their front door white, grey or yellow. *East* facing houses can paint their front door green or purple. Houses that face *south, south-west,* and *north-east* can benefit from a red front door.

6) *What does it mean if a stairway is facing the front door? Does this stop the energy?*

   This is not good energy as the natural chi energy rushes to either the lower or the higher floor, thus leaving the main floor without feng shui nourishment. As a cure, I would place a small wind chime at the bottom of the stairway, or vase of flowers on a piece of furniture, or a small hanging crystal to stop the flow from escaping.

7) *If I think I have spirits in my home blocking my natural energy. What can I do and can they harm me?*

   Earthbound spirits or lost spirits in the home cannot hurt you. Usually, they are lost in the astral plane, and in most cases, are more afraid of you as they usually have no understanding that they are actually dead. They certainly will cause a lot of problems though. If this is the case give the home a good smudging immediately as I have described in this book. Do this for several days as it will usually send them packing. The smell of the sage and gum leaves usually makes them feel sick, and will also clear away any negative energy in the home as well. Once you have finished smudging your home, your space will feel lighter, clearer, and more harmonious. Any unpleasant smells of a paranormal nature will disappear and your home will be comfortable and liveable again. If you still have problems, you need to send for an experienced medium that does rescue work to help cross them over once and for all.

8) *How do I know if my home does not feel right?*

Always trust your own judgement and intuition as this is your gift from spirit and heaven, and you are always right when you trust your own feelings, which can only empower you. Anyone can learn to work with feng shui, as it is something you can play with and learn as you go along, but you must remember that it takes years of practice and there are many layers in traditional feng shui that are quite complicated. Practice makes perfect as they say, so why not learn this ancient art to improve every possible aspect of your life?

9) *Are you having problems selling a home?*

Every day, I get asked by people why their house isn't selling, or the business moving along faster. Try these quick tips and without a doubt you will get a positive result.

1. Clear all the clutter. When you clear clutter from your home, you are removing negative, blocked energy. This simple procedure will not only bring more balance and harmony in your life but it will help in the sale of the home and allow you to move on. Just like spring-cleaning, but on an energetic level, space clearing releases negative energy and encourages positive energy to enter our lives, because often as consumers we collect a lot of things that we truly don't need that can block the natural flow of energy.

2. Give your home a good smoke out with some dried gum leaves and sage, which you can burn in an old tin. Once you have done this, room by room, it will disperse any negative energy and help any souls or spirits move on that may be lost or stuck on the astral. After a while you will intuitively feel the energy in your home feels a lot lighter. Lost souls or spirits can disturb the natural balances of a home and create incredible disturbances, which in turn stops the natural flow of good chi energy. Family members can get sick, pets will be affected, and it will be impossible to sell or rent the home, as all the natural good energy will be drained.

3. Once you feel satisfied with what you have done, light a candle inside the front door, walk around the space, room by room, and talk to your home or space, in a loving, compassionate way, and say that you have been grateful for its protection, shelter and love. When you have done this, tell the home softly that you are ready to move on and thank it again for the experiences, love and gratitude it gave you, your family, or your clients if this was a business while living there.

10) *How can I be successful and make a difference in the world?*

Most successful people in the world are driven by love, kindness, inspiration, and creativity, and absolutely LOVE what they do. They are passionate about their work, their ideas, and feel they want to and can make a difference in the world. They would never cheat, lie or behave in a bad way towards others, as they understand the law of karma. What goes around comes around. They also understand how important it is to praise people and not criticise others, as just like a flower we all need to be nurtured and watered and bathed in light so we can grow and reach our highest potential. I also believe it is a good thing to give back to others or have a charity where you can make a difference in the world for people less fortunate than yourself. Another good way is to stay positive and focused, no matter what you are going through, never compare yourself to others and remember that things happen for a reason in the general scheme of things. And most importantly, walk away from negative people or gossips, as these energies are highly toxic to the soul, on another vibration, and learning their own lessons, in their own way.

# Recommended Reading

The Power of Now – Eckhart Tolle

How To Win Friends and Influence People – Dale Carnegie

Life is Awesome – Roxanne

The Beginner's Guide to Wealth – Noel Whittaker

Numerology – Thomas Muldoon

Feng Shui – George Birdsall

Make This Your Lucky Day – Ellen Whitehurst

Stuffed to Sorted – Mary Anne Bennie

Sorted – Lissanne Oliver

Joyful Voices – Doris Stokes

The Physics of Angels – Mathew Fox and Rupert Sheldrake

Crystal Power, Crystal Healing – Michael Gienger

Feng Shui – Eva Wong

Spirits Whispering In My Ear – Kerrie Erwin

Magical Tales of the Forrest – Kerrie Erwin

Sacred Soul – Kerrie Erwin

Tarot for Light Workers – Kerrie Erwin

Memoirs of a Suburban Medium – Kerrie Erwin

SPIRITUAL MEDIUM, CLAIRVOYANT AND INTERNATIONAL AUTHOR

**Kerrie Erwin**

**www.pureview.com.au**

Sydney-based medium Kerrie Erwin has lived between two worlds since childhood and is able to *see, smell, sense,* and *hear* spirit people talking. Realising her true calling when she was very young, she now works professionally as a spiritual medium and clairvoyant, conducts spirit rescues, investigates hauntings, and connects people to loved ones that have passed over into the spirit world. She also teaches metaphysics, reads tarot cards, and works with feng shui. She is trained in spiritual hypnotherapies and past-life regression. She has her own office in Roseville and works via phone, Skype, and other media, all over Australia.

Closely aligned to her healing work is Kerrie's vibrant creative nature, she regularly works on stage and in spiritualist churches around the country. Kerrie has also written several books, works on different radio shows as a guest speaker, and is a highly sought-after writer. She has written many well-publicised articles on the paranormal over the years.

She has also hosted her own show on cable TV called *Let's Have a Chat with Kerrie,* and worked for two years on Psychic TV. Her aim as a spiritual medium is to help as many people as possible, to teach others that love is eternal, to grow and to inspire others to believe in themselves.

She is the author of *Magical Tales of the Forest, Memoirs of a Suburban Medium, Spirits Whispering in my Ear, Tarot for Light Workers and Sacred Soul.* These books are available to buy on her website, at selected bookstores, and on Kindle and Amazon.

*Other products by Kerrie...*

ISBN: 978-0-992307-02-8

SACRED SOUL

*'When you truly surrender your love, soul and spirit to the work that you were meant to do, spirit will always look after you. Not only will you have food on your table, a roof over your head but your life will always be full of love and you will never be alone.'*

A truly good and easy read, this is Kerrie's fifth book to date and is based on not only true-life case studies, but also spiritual wisdom, healing tips and enjoyable stories documented from ordinary working medium living in downtown Sydney with a busy practise. It is quite different from most paranormal books as it is entertaining, educational and informative and most readers around the globe will be able to relate to some of the extraordinary situations and topics, Kerrie explains and talks about in her stories with great detail, but never had the courage to talk about.

While most people have no idea of the spirit world, this book will, without a doubt open people's minds and help them understand that the loving spirit world does indeed exist, there is another world beyond us and that the soul never dies, but lives on. Not only will Kerrie take you on an adventure into the spiritual world of hauntings, healings, reincarnation and incredible phenomena, you will learn and understand about topics, that may be controversial to most people but learn that there is nothing ever to fear, as fear is just the unknown and love is always eternal.

Available from all bookstores and online.